The Man Who Brought Brodsky into English

The Man Who Brought Brodsky into English

Conversations with George L. Kline

BOSTON
2021

Library of Congress Cataloging-in-Publication Data

Names: Haven, Cynthia L., interviewer. | Kline, George L. (George Louis),
    1921-2014, interviewee. | Polukhina, Valentina, writer of afterword.
Title: The man who brought Brodsky into English : conversations with George
    L. Kline / Cynthia L. Haven ; with an afterword by Valentina Polukhina.
Other titles: Jews of Russia & Eastern Europe and their legacy.
Description: Boston : Academic Studies Press, 2020. | Series: Jews of
    Russia & Eastern Europe and their legacy | Includes bibliographical
    references.
Identifiers: LCCN 2020038964 (print) | LCCN 2020038965 (ebook) | ISBN
    9781644695135 (hardback) | ISBN 9781644695142 (paperback) | ISBN
    9781644695159 (adobe pdf) | ISBN 9781644695166 (epub)
Subjects: LCSH: Kline, George L. (George Louis), 1921-2014--Interviews. |
    Brodsky, Joseph, 1940-1996. | Brodsky, Joseph, 1940-1996--Translations
    into English. | Translators--United States--Interviews. | Russian
    poetry--20th century--Translations into English.
Classification: LCC PG3479.4.R64 Z684 2020 (print) | LCC PG3479.4.R64
    (ebook) | DDC 891.71/44--dc23
LC record available at https://lccn.loc.gov/2020038964
LC ebook record available at https://lccn.loc.gov/2020038965

Book design by Lapiz Digital Services
Cover design by Zoë Patrick. On the cover: Joseph Brodsky and George
Kline share a joke during a reading at the University of Virginia,
Charlottesville, February 21, 1974. (Photo: Andre Berkin, Bryn Mawr
Special Collections, Bryn Mawr, PA)

Published by Academic Studies Press
1577 Beacon Street
Brookline, MA 02446, USA
press@academicstudiespress.com
www.academicstudiespress.com

George L. Kline, Bryn Mawr's Milton C. Nahm Professor of Philosophy, at his desk in 1987. (Photo: Ron Tarver, *Philadelphia Inquirer*)

In memory of George L. Kline, with gratitude

Contents

Introduction:
To Please Two Shadows

George L. Kline translated more of Nobel laureate Joseph Brodsky's poems than any other single person, with the exception of Brodsky himself. He described himself to me as "Brodsky's first serious translator." Bryn Mawr's Milton C. Nahm Professor of Philosophy was a modest and retiring man, but on occasion he could be as forthright and adamant as Brodsky himself. In a 1994 letter, the Slavic scholar wrote: "Akhmatova discovered Brodsky for Russia, but I discovered him for the West."[1] And in 1987, "I was the first in the West to recognize him as a major poet, and the first to translate his work *in extenso*."[2] It was all true. He was, moreover, one of the few translators who was a fluent Russian speaker.

Brodsky's first book in America, 1973's *Joseph Brodsky: Selected Poems*,[3] changed my life as well as the poet's—and all the translations were Kline's. The meditative poems of time, consciousness, suffering, alienation, even redemption sounded a note that was octaves above the free-form narcissism, the weary story of the self that typified American poetry at the time. This book established a Western audience for Brodsky, and blew open a window to the East. I studied with him at the University of Michigan, and that was a formative experience, too, as it was for so many of his protégées who became writers in his wake.

---

1   G.L. Kline to Marc Boots-Ebenfield, 1994—from George Kline's private papers.
2   G.L. Kline to Christina Nylander, November 24, 1987—from George Kline's private papers.
3   Joseph Brodsky, *Joseph Brodsky: Selected Poems* (Harmondsworth: Penguin, 1973). Harper & Row published a hardback edition the following January.

This is the story of how that book was born, and what happened in the years following. The three-decade collaboration of Kline and Brodsky is a tale that has not been told in its entirety until now.

The first translation one reads of a foreign poet makes an indelible impression, and so I confess a bias, since Kline's translations were the first that I read. But my preference wasn't wholly subjective; and I wasn't alone—they made an impression on the entire Anglophone world. They also launched a stunning, unconventional literary career in the West for Brodsky. In the years since, his translations have sometimes been disparaged, often for the occasional infelicity, though few translations lack them. (Kline was considering a new edition of the *Selected* at the end of his life, which would have included his corrections and newer translations. It never happened.) More often they were simply overlooked as more famous poets and translators took on the task. He was obviously not a superstar poet—such as Richard Wilbur, or Seamus Heaney, or Anthony Hecht, who also translated Brodsky's poetry although they didn't know Russian—but rather a Slavic scholar with a serious interest in poetry. This book shows how deep this philosopher's commitment was, and that these poems were not the whimsy of a dilettante. His translations were important not only because they were the first, but because they tried to preserve, as Brodsky wished,

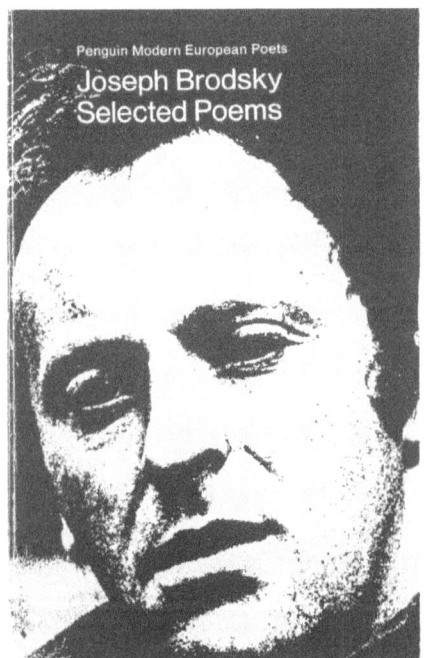

the metrical and rhyme schemes of the original, often with surprising sensitivity and success.

As I pored over the book with the stylized green-and-purple portrait on the cover as a university student, I knew nothing of the translator, George L. Kline. Yet the book, the man, and the poet would be one of the more remarkable adventures of my life. The three of us formed an unlikely troika of temperaments and training, friendship and estrangements. George was meticulous, reserved, and deeply principled; Brodsky was an evident genius, a Catherine wheel of a man, who fraternized with the leading cultural figures of his time. The two were lucky to have found each other; yet their personalities were worlds apart. I entered the scene writing about both men decades later, undoubtedly one of the girls described in Brodsky's 1972 poem "In the Lake District," the place where he had been appointed "to wear out the patience of the ingenuous local youth."

Though we had never met face to face, George would become a regular presence in my life. The connection began after my publication of 2003's *Joseph Brodsky: Conversations,* my carte d'entrée to the world of Brodsky scholarship. After the book was out, I received a multi-page letter with "corrigenda." I later learned that anyone in the world who wrote or published something about Joseph Brodsky could expect such a patient, careful list of corrections. He was thorough, neutral, scholarly— welcoming and encour-aging, too.

According to his colleague Philip Grier, writing in the *Slavic Review,*[4] "George Kline was an exceptional exemplar of *humanitas*: kindness, culture, refinement." Brodsky scholar Zakhar Ishov told me that Kline "was a *decent man*," and not in the bland and neutered sense of the term, but in the sense of an endangered species.

Wherever we are, at whatever stage of our journey, those who work with Brodsky's corpus owe him a great debt. So do translators more generally. He encouraged every scholar and translator, no matter how new and ill-equipped for the job at hand.[5] When he was invited to judge the Compass Translation Competition, held under the auspices of the *Cardinal Points Journal,* his letter to Russian poet and translator Irina Mashinski signaled his magnanimity and sense of fairness. On January 21, 2012, he wrote to her:

> As you may know, in the past, film awards (both Golden Globes and Oscars) were announced with the formula 'And the winner is . . .'. However, in recent years, for good reason, this has been changed to 'And the Golden Globe [or Oscar] goes to. . . .' The Russian *pobeditel'* that you used last year is even stronger than 'winner'; to me it suggests that those who didn't get the prize were not only 'losers' but 'defeated ones.' Why not say simply 'Congratulations on the selection of your translation'? And to the others 'We regret that your translation

4   Philip T. Grier, "George L. Kline, 1921–2014," *Slavic Review* 74, no. 1 (2015): 233–35.
5   He also encouraged me to collaborate with him on an ambitious translation of "Conversations with an Angel"—a wholly unexpected honor, but one that never came to pass, given our preexisting professional commitments.

was not chosen'? Both of these formulas would soften the harsh image of competitiveness that is implied by the language of 'winners' and 'losers.'

The Man Who Brought Brodsky Into English: Conversations with George Kline is a tribute and a gift from all of us, winners, losers, and the rest of us.

***

As the years went by, I would occasionally phone George Kline at Christmas. Every year I would get his detailed family holiday letter. It touched lightly on George's professional work, including instead family news, recent travels, and health updates for his family, especially his beloved wife Ginny and "Bunny," the Klines' disabled daughter. For news of his scholarly labor (he was revising this or that essay, publishing a new study), I would have to follow up by phone to Anderson, South Carolina, where he had retired.

In 2012, I made the seasonal call. We hadn't talked for a while, so we updated each other on our articles and books. After a short conversation, he abruptly announced the end of our chat with unexpected firmness: "I've got to go."

"Sure, George. But why?"

"We've been talking for twelve minutes."

"Yes. So?"

Then he said with slow emphasis: "*I am ninety-two, you know.*"

No. I didn't know. How would I? We had never met. I couldn't even recall seeing a photo of George. I knew he was getting on, but I didn't have a mental picture of this nonagenarian who was, actually, a few months shy of his ninety-second birthday.

I had always meant to gather his memories. But at that point in my life I had just embarked on the book that became *Evolution of Desire: A Life of René Girard,* a biography of the French theorist and personal friend. I had also just launched an innovative communications program at Stanford. However, I knew it would be foolhardy to postpone any longer. Not only for my sake, but for the benefit of scholars around the world who had been guided by his tutelage, improved by his impeccable corrections and guidance, and inspired by his meticulous standards.

We began our work together in January 2013. I was interviewing a man in failing health, who was only capable of conversations of up to twenty minutes in the morning, while he was still fresh. (Some days he couldn't talk at all, and on one banner morning we talked for about forty minutes.) We couldn't wait for a better time. With characteristic stoicism, he was adapting to the possible, not pining for the ideal. We both sensed it would be the only opportunity.

Over the subsequent months, our interviews filled hundreds of pages. The work was "exhilarating, but often challenging and exhausting," he wrote in a letter to Ishov. Much of our conversation was repetitious, chit-chat about peripheral people or events, discussions of his health or arranging the next telephone rendezvous, but over the months, I would learn of his courage and his sense of honor, as well as the precision of his scholarship. In the Brodsky world of intellectual brilliance and acrobatic language, George's conversations, occasionally punctuated with stiff little jokes that ended with flat punchlines (he'd sometimes repeat them to drive the point home), would seem to make him the odd man out. He was there, he would say, because he didn't have "a poet's ego," and he could work from the original Russian, and did not attempt to impose his own forms on the formal cadences, rhymes and slant rhymes, and complicated metrical structures of the original. I also learned of his patience and his peevishness. I began to sense in this staid Unitarian a profound religiosity beneath the surface, and that he shared with the poet a sacred vision of the world. And I came to know his wounded pride.

In our conversations, he described his meeting with the poet who would change his life, his run-ins with the notorious KGB, and other untold or little-known details of his friendship with Brodsky. He spoke about the poet's generosity in 1974, when he was "disinvited" from giving a reading at Italy's Spoleto Festival because of Soviet blackmail. Or the "White Nights" in June 1968, when Brodsky rented a rowboat and took Kline down the Fontanka in the early hours of the morning. Or in October 1987, when Brodsky's Nobel Prize was announced, and Kline phoned him in London to say "Congratulations, Joseph!" Brodsky responded, "And congratulations to you, too, George!"

I also learned more fully about his heroism, a subject we touched on in our interviews, though his modesty deterred him from giving a full account of his bravery. During World War II, as a navigator and bombardier in

B-24s, he flew fifty important combat missions out of Italy, for which he received the Distinguished Flying Cross.

He described how, as Brodsky insisted more and more on his own translations, he eventually seemed to leave the Russian scholar behind, favoring the work of other translators and, Kline thought, dismissing him as intractable. He had, to some extent, anticipated this. Even before Brodsky's arrival in the United States, the scholar had written in a letter, "I'm not a possessive translator, and I'm convinced that others some day will translate Brodsky more successfully than I've been able to do. I welcome pluralism in the Englishing of any foreign poet."[6] Although Kline felt slighted, the friendship continued till the end, as did their work together. Kline attended his final birthday party months before the poet's death.

As we persevered, a more ambitious goal developed. We began to hope these conversations would be edited and pruned into a book to complete the oral history of Joseph Brodsky, so comprehensively undertaken by Valentina Polukhina in *Brodsky through the Eyes of His Contemporaries*. George Kline was one of the few major figures in Brodsky's life who had not been interviewed for the volumes.

We were running out of time. The phone calls—punctuated by constant sips of water to keep him going; sometimes he was breathing audibly—gradually yielded to longer breaks in the conversation to check on the well-being of his beloved wife or daughter. As his energy was fading, he was urging me to use his earlier articles to augment our interviews, since our conversations were missing strategic parts of the story.

But the future was vaporizing. Ginny was hospitalized, and once more George had to put our plans on ice, as he took care of the household and attended his wife and met other professional deadlines. When she died on April 5, 2014, the life seemed to go out of George. His health declined precipitously, all the while he kept saying he would return to our project soon. He died six months later, on October 21.

Our collaborative project to please a shadow was now mine alone. And now I must please two shadows.

***

---

6 Letter to Elizabeth Kray, executive director of the Academy of American Poets, July 2, 1972—from George Kline's private papers.

It was only after his death that I fully realized the stature of the man. So many of us focused on his high-profile work with the celebrity poet Brodsky that we didn't realize his importance as a scholar of Russian philosophy and culture. "His personal presence in our midst was a gift, not to be replaced; his influence on the field is by now indelible," wrote Grier.[7]

He published more than 300 articles, chapters in anthologies, encyclopedia entries, book reviews, review articles, and, of course, translations. He authored two monographs and edited or coedited six anthologies. He wrote authoritative studies of Hegel, Spinoza, and Whitehead, and made notable contributions to understanding Marx and Marxism. He inspired a generation of younger scholars, poets, and translators—including Ishov and Mashinski, the two who were able to keep up with his exacting, tireless correspondence. What's lesser known is how greatly this quiet Bryn Mawr professor supported scholars around the world who were working with Russian poetry and Brodsky in particular.

The Kline family encouraged me to continue with the project that had been interrupted by the death of its subject and collaborator. They were generous with their help in a time of great family upheaval and trauma. At my request, several big boxes of articles, drafts, translations, correspondence, emails, newspaper clippings, photos, and more arrived at my Palo Alto home. The family's graciousness during a time of stress was much appreciated.

With these records, and my transcripts and notes, I continued our conversation post-mortem—in some ways easier, without the crackling of bad Skype connections and accumulating mp3 files, without the exhaustion, the background noise of domestic emergencies that had became increasingly frequent and urgent. In other ways the task had become harder, too, as I became the editor of a unique fragment of literary history, as well as the interlocutor within it. As George had wished, I blended our conversations with other material to fill in vital parts of his story, adding an additional layer of complexity to an already complicated project. Over the weeks and months, I transformed our brief, piecemeal talks into the conversations we *could* have shared, had time and circumstances allowed.

---

7   Grier, "George L. Kline, 1921–2014," 233–35.

I relied on a vast range of articles, interviews, letters, emails, and other records. With one of the boxes the family had sent, filled with his tiny 2.5" x 3" datebooks, I could confirm appointments from the crabbed, often inscrutable penciled scrawls on the fading pages. I pored over the holdings at Yale's Beinecke Library, which holds many of his important papers. My fondest hope is that I have included enough to restore the legacy of an overlooked figure in the Brodsky circle, a man who has not gotten his due.

I remember the sting of his criticism, and came to wonder if there was any translation that he truly liked without qualification; he criticized even close friends. Yet I found among his papers his generous appraisal of me for a 2007 National Endowment of the Humanities application: "I always read Cynthia's writings with real pleasure; they are uniformly concise, lively, and richly informative. Poet Kay Ryan noted perceptively that Cynthia's writing about poetry 'has the sting and bite of poetry in it.' This is high praise, but strikes me as fully justified. As an editor she is unusually conscientious, persistent, and resourceful." My road was longer without this kindly scholar prodding me onward.

During the initial phase of the project, we received funding from the Andrew W. Mellon Foundation, under the aegis of Bryn Mawr. Much later, after George's death, Valentina Polukhina took the project under her aegis and was able to get British Academy support for the effort. As a consequence, Valentina and I spent a week together at her home in Golders Green in March 2018, carefully combing through the final manuscript. We got to know each other much better, and her proofreading, feedback, and fine-tuning of the manuscript—and her overarching knowledge of Brodsky's work and life—were crucial.

One of Joseph Brodsky's remarkable gifts was the caliber of the people he attracted around him. As George told me, "He was very good at—how shall I put it?—judging people and feeling almost at first contact that they were good people, serious people, intelligent, knowledgeable, perceptive, and he wanted to be with them, to be their friends. There weren't very many people like that." He cited the instant rapport with Seamus Heaney, Derek Walcott, Mark Strand, Dick Wilbur, Susan Sontag, and Bob Silvers, and "probably a couple of others that I've forgotten." One of the people he had forgotten was, of course, himself. Steadfast, meticulous, and quietly loyal George is usually not mentioned with this crowd. But he had qualities many of us couldn't touch.

Later, the Russian poet was asked, "When you first came to the United States, what surprised you most? It's been said that you drew some of your expectations from reading Robert Frost, that you felt America would be more rural than you found it." He replied, "Not more rural, but I thought that the people would be less vocal, less hysterical, more reserved, more prudent with their speech."[8] Surely he found those very qualities of restraint and dignity in the man he had met way back in Leningrad, August 1967, who would become his first serious translator.

During the time we were doing our interviews, George had suggested this sentence from writer Igor Yefimov for an epigraph: "Everyone who had any connection with Joseph Brodsky knows that he is doomed to think and talk about the poet to his own final day."[9] Then he added, "It would apply to both of us, after all."

---

8   David Montenegro, "An Interview with Joseph Brodsky," in *Joseph Brodsky: Conversations*, ed. Cynthia L. Haven (Jackson: University Press of Mississippi, 2002), 117.

9   "Kazhdyi, kto byl sviazan s Brodskim, znaet, chto dumat' i govorit' o nëm on obrechën do kontsa dnei svoikh" (Igor Yefimov, *Nobelevskii tuneiadets* [The Nobel parasite] [Moscow: Zakharov, 2005]). This passage is taken from the back cover of the book.

Chapter 1

A Love Affair with Language

You have translated the Nobel poet Joseph Brodsky, but also Anna Akhmatova, Marina Tsvetaeva, Boris Pasternak, and others—frequently to acclaim. Russia became your lifelong passion, but it was a love, oddly enough, born in Germany. Tell us that story.

I had three years of high school German, and was already reading German poetry by the time I reached college. I still think Goethe's lyric poems are about the best in any language.

Also, my first teacher of Russian, in a spring semester after the war, was André von Gronicka, a professor of German Literature. I first finished my undergraduate studies at Columbia College. He was born in Moscow of a Baltic German father and a Russian mother. He was fully trilingual, and his English was near-native. Later, I took his wonderful course on Goethe and Schiller.

So my love affair with Russian poetry goes back a long way, to my years as a graduate student at Columbia University in New York, from 1947 to 1949.

At some point during these years, around 1947, I began to translate from Russian. The first piece I published was a short story, two or three pages long, by Mikhail Zoshchenko. It's a wonderful story. Maybe if I can find it I'll send it to you.

Zoshchenko is hilarious, and of course his underlying tone of despair and sadness makes him a kind of a modern Gogol. I met his widow once. I made it a point to go to where she was living just a year or two after he had died. I think it was in '56. She liked to say that he was a Gogol of our time. That was not verse translation, of course, but rather prose.

Perhaps inevitably, the first Russian poet I read and fell in love with was Pushkin. I don't recall trying to translate any poem by Goethe or Schiller. I started instead with Pushkin, as early as 1947 or 1948. When I began my graduate studies in Columbia at that time, a few of us got together to form a small *kruzhok.* I began in Slavic Studies, and only later switched to philosophy.

What was the first poem of his that you translated?

I think my first attempt was "Ia vas liubil. Liubov′ eshchë, byt′ mozhet, / V dushe moei ugasla ne sovsem." As I recall, I rendered it: "I loved you once. And in my heart still lingers, / Not wholly quenched by time, that love's first flame." I couldn't finish it in the way I wanted, so I gave it up.

Even in the very beginning, I tried to keep the metric pattern of the original, and where I could, without padding and artificialities. I tried to keep the rhyme scheme. Meter always came first.

Despite that unpromising beginning, you persisted.

I published translations of two of Pasternak's early poems in 1959. Eventually, I collected them into a small *knizhka,* called *Boris Pasternak: Seven Poems.* In six I was able to keep Pasternak's meter. iambic tetrameter or pentameter, and in one four-foot amphibrachs. Most English and American translators have rendered amphibrachs as English iambics. I still resist that widespread tendency.

I guess you could call this syllable counting, but I don't think of it that way, but rather as feeling and hearing the rhythm of the original and trying to replicate it in English.

By that time, you were at Bryn Mawr, where you continued to pursue your dual loves, philosophy and literature.

Yes. During my first four years at Bryn Mawr, from 1959 to 1964, about two-thirds of my teaching was in the philosophy department, and about a third in the Russian department. I regularly taught courses in Russian philosophy, but also courses in Russian literature of the late nineteenth and twentieth centuries. This included a good deal of poetry—Blok, Mayakovsky, Yesenin, Akhmatova, Pasternak, and Tsvetaeva. Later I added Mandelstam. I had loved poetry for many years—English, German, Russian, and even Italian.

Over the years, I taught courses not only in philosophy, but history, even ethics. In my single year at Chicago, I taught a course called, "Great Books of the Western World from Homer to Dostoevsky." It was wonderful, and full of poetry, some of which I was encountering for the first time. I think that's probably where I first encountered Dante and fell instantly in love.

Your publication of Pasternak's poems, which coincided with your arrival at Bryn Mawr, where you would spend the rest of your career, occurred only five years before you encountered the work of Joseph Brodsky, shortly after his 1964 trial. And that work would become the culmination of your career as a translator. You'd come a long way since those classes in Russian with a German professor.

I sent Gronicka a copy of the *Selected Poems* I'd translated. He replied with a lovely letter, writing, "I don't usually read English translations of Russian poetry with any pleasure, but yours of Brodsky are a delight. You two are truly *wahlverwandt.* That's an old German expression meaning an "elective affinity." It was a phrase that Goethe used, of course.

And surely it applies to your love for the Russian language as well. Let's discuss the first chapter in your long partnership with the top Russian poet of the postwar generation.

Chapter 2

The Leningrad Poet and "a gift fit for a king"

How did you first hear about Joseph Brodsky?

I had never heard of him before his Kafkaesque Leningrad trial in early 1964. When I first began to visit the Soviet Union in 1956, he was a teenager, and hadn't even started to write poetry.

By the time of my second and third visits, in 1957 and 1960, he had written several poems, but none of them found their way into the samizdat I was reading.

During that time, he said he had started to write verse because he had read "a quite remarkable Soviet poet—Boris Slutsky."[1] Both poets experimented with form, mixing street language with formal diction, and weaving Old Testament threads into their verse.[2]

During that time also, he was already getting arrested and jailed. Yet although he had fallen out with the Soviet regime—or rather vice versa—he was at peace with his Soviet peers, and he looked at the poetry, not the political affiliation of the poet. A Leningrad friend, the geologist and volcanologist

---

1 Brodsky's Interview with Annie Epelboin, cited in Mikhail Meilakh, "Liberation from Emotionality," in *Brodsky through the Eyes of His Contemporaries*, 2 vols., ed. Valentina Polukhina (Boston: Academic Studies Press, 2004), 1:211n1.

2 Though Brodsky would come to these Old Testament themes a little later. He first read the Bible in 1963 and wrote "Isaac and Abraham" within the first few days after reading Genesis.

Genrikh Steinberg, said, "He was not a typical dissident, but he did not fit in with those in power. He was different, but they did not understand this: a binary system: 'black/white, even/odd,' 'who is not with us, he is . . . ,' and so forth. Joseph, by the way, had nothing but good words for Slutsky and Okudzhava"³—both were Communists. I understand that later, in America, he would call Okudzhava a mediocrity. So when did you see the first poems?

By the August after the trial in February and March of 1964, I had run across one or two very short poems, and they were published with the transcript of the trial in *The New Leader*, among other places.

Frida Vigdorova's bootlegged transcript of that trial was certainly a riveting international debut for him.

The transcript and poems made it clear that he was a bold and independent spirit, grossly abused by his government. But the translations, which were inadequate, didn't give any indication whether he was an important poet.

But you discovered his poetry through a friend.

Yes. I was in Eastern Europe for a total of two months. I went to libraries to see what they had in the way of interesting Russians like Pasternak. I eventually met Seweryn Pollak, the distinguished Polish critic and translator of Akhmatova and Pasternak, who invited me to meet him.

From your datebook, it looks like that happened on December 20, 1964—a Sunday.

It was just before Christmas. We were talking in Russian about the older poets he had met, of course I knew none of them. I almost met Pasternak once, but didn't, and he was dead by '64. After a half an hour or more of discussion in his study about the older poets—he had known many of them personally—he suddenly asked me what I thought of the younger poets. And I asked, "Which ones?" He said, "Well, for example, this Joseph Brodsky?" I told him what I knew about him, which was so very little about

---

3   Genrikh Steinberg, "Joseph Wanted to Know Everything," in Polukhina, *Brodsky through the Eyes of His Contemporaries*, 2: 132.

his poetry, and he said, "Well, I have something here." He turned to this great pile of papers on his desk. He shuffled around and got half-way down the stack and pulled out a faint carbon copy on onionskin paper—third or fourth carbon copies, so it wasn't terribly clear, but they were legible, typed manuscripts.

It was "The Great Elegy for John Donne," from 1963. It knocked me over. All these years later, I still recall vividly the opening lines of that powerful poem and of the passages at the end of it that I managed to scan quickly on the spot. I only had ten minutes to look at it, but I knew by the time I'd read six lines that he was a great Russian poet. It was a moment of revelation.

These passages struck me as a kind of revelation or epiphany:

> John Donne has sunk in sleep . . . All things beside
> are sleeping too: walls, bed, and floor—all sleep.
> The table, pictures, carpets, hooks, and bolts,
> clothes-closets, cupboards, candles, curtains—all
> now sleep: the washbowl, bottle, tumbler, bread,
> breadknife and china, crystal, pots and pans . . .

and this—

> Like some great bird, he too will wake at dawn;
> but now he lies beneath a veil of white,
> while snow and sleep stitch up the throbbing void
> between his soul and his own dreaming flesh.

(trans. George L. Kline)

Were you able to take a copy with you back to the United States?

No. In those days, the copying equipment was pretty primitive. I didn't even try to copy it.

So you left Warsaw without it, a few days later, and got back to the United States around Christmas time, 1964.

But the poem continued to haunt me. I wrote to some knowledgeable friends to see if I could track it down—Victor Erlich at Yale and Max Hayward at St. Anthony's College at Oxford. Max is a distinguished translator of Sinyavsky, Pasternak, and later Nadezhda Mandelstam. I also wrote to a notable translator of Voznesensky—Vera Sandomirsky Dunham at Wayne State University. Vera sent me the copy of the Great Elegy that she had received from her Moscow contacts late in February 1965. Did you ever meet her?

No.

She was a very engaging and energetic personality. Lots of fun to listen to and speak with. She had received a complete text. There were some bad misprints in it, but it was a complete text. She received it a couple weeks after I got back to the states. Early in 1965, I got the text and started translating it immediately.

I had completed my own translation of that poem within a matter of weeks. It was published in Northwestern's *TriQuarterly* in the spring of 1965, along with several shorter ones.

Soon you returned to the USSR.

I was in Russia only briefly. I had planned to stay longer and I may have even tried to meet Brodsky, but that visit, in July 1966, had to be cut short because of my daughter's illness, so I never got to Leningrad.

This was the only time she had traveled with us. She was spending her junior year in France. I met her—where was it? In Antwerp I guess.

According to your datebook, it was on Sunday, July 10. Brussels, though of course you may have traveled from there to Antwerp.

We flew into Moscow together. She began to get ill on her twentieth birthday on July 16. It turned out to be multiple sclerosis. So I had a desperate time with the doctors, and eventually we just had to cut the whole trip short and fly back.

It was a nightmare ordeal for you, George. A tragedy that changed your family forever. I admire how much you and your wife Ginny, as well as the rest of your family, have been loving, heroic, and self-sacrificing with your care of Bunny, then and ever since.

Yet you persevered in your trips to Russia and your support of the young poet. A year later, in August 1967, you went back to Leningrad for the first time since 1960. And that's when you finally met Joseph.

I had mailed him an offprint of my revised version of "Elegy for John Donne," published in the *Russian Review* in October 1965. I gave him my hotel and room number as a return address. Three days later, at 1:30 a.m., the telephone jangled me awake. It was Brodsky, of course, inviting me to visit him at his apartment.

I arrived at his famous "room-and-a-half" later that day. His first words to me—as I stretched out my hand to grasp his through the open door—were "Cherez porog nel'zia" ("Don't greet anyone across the threshold"). He smiled and quickly added in heavily accented English, that it was "old Russian custom." I confess I had rehearsed the first words I said to him—but they are no less sincere for that. "Meeting you at this moment is, for me, like meeting the twenty-seven-year-old Anna Akhmatova in 1916, the twenty-seven-year-old Boris Pasternak in 1917, or the twenty-seven-year-old Marina Tsvetaeva in 1919." I should have added "and the twenty-seven-year-old Osip Mandelstam in 1918," but in 1967, I'm ashamed to admit, I had not come to know and cherish Mandelstam's poetry.

Those were the same words you would later use in the closing paragraphs of your graceful introduction to the Selected. *You ended, "Whether Joseph Brodsky will one day stand beside these four giants of twentieth-century Russian poetry it is perhaps still too early to say. I myself am confident he will." It's not too early to say now, and you stand by it.*

I do.

But let's go back to that first meeting. What you were expecting to see when that door opened? I mean, had you formed any expectations or seen any photos?

I had never seen a photograph of him at that point. Well, he was quite good-looking, as you know. I do remember asking him, "How old are you?"

He had a great reverence for age, partly because some of the older critics who had mentored him about Russian metrics and prosody. Anyway, he announced "twenty-seven." And then he immediately added with a wry smile, "I'm sorry it's so few." Meaning so few years. Later he said to somebody, "Well, my translator is almost fifty". I wasn't, but I was forty-six. That seemed old to him, and something to revere.

You said you were excited. What excited you about this meeting?

Oh, I was excited to meet him. I was already excited about the poems of his that I'd seen. Of course I was thrilled to be meeting him and talking to him. I mean, as you know, he was charismatic. That came through in our first couple hours of conversation.

I don't remember our conversation, obviously we talked about his poetry.

The first of many meetings. How often did you meet after that?

Almost daily for the next week, and for several days in early September, also, when I was in Leningrad again.

But already in these early days, the two of you attracted "official" attention.

He planned to show me the Fontanny Dom, which had been the residence of Akhmatova. A "KGBeast" started trailing us as we walked through the streets of Leningrad. Joseph showered the man with powerful Russian profanity, and we had to give up the project.

He had already had a good deal of experience with KGBeasts.

Joseph was first picked up and interrogated by the KGB because he had published in the underground almanac *Sintaksis* in 1960.[4]

So the KGB was a colorful early note to your friendship. And then you took your leave.

His parting words to me were usually "Don't change"—this, in English, or later "Khrani Vas Bog, Dzhordzh" ("May God keep you, George").

Interesting. This seems more than a formulaic greeting for a Soviet citizen. Yet this is the man who wrote the poem that ends "the only touch of bliss/that's open to a village atheist."
   Something else happened during those years that doesn't get talked about much—a direct experience that his Soviet upbringing hadn't give him a language or context to describe. From a 1988 interview in America:

---

4   In Russia, an "almanac" is a literary anthology issued once a year or more infrequently.

Q.: You've said that you have been given two or three revelations in your life.
A.: Yeah, well, two or three, yeah. Well, it's actually a private matter, obviously. Fancy me talking about revelations. The reason I never told about them to anyone is simply because I thought, "Well, next thing will happen to me is I'll be locked up." Also, they took place when I was rather young, well, I was 22, 23.[5] And I thought, "Well, if I'm going to mention that, well, some Jeanne d'Arc deal will . . ."

Q.: This is certainly an age that doesn't put too much stock in people who claim to have revelations.
A.: Stupid of them, of the age.

Q.: What does one know after a revelation that one doesn't know before?
A.: Ah. Sensible question. One gets certain that one is doing right. Because affirmation comes from so far away, it's almost like—how shall I put it?—it's simply that somebody cares to instruct you from the bowels of the universe. You sense that somebody bothered about you out there in that great infinity. Actually, both times that I had those moments which I regard as revelations, I had some sort of astronomical illumination, yeah? And I guess I'm actually rather distressed that they cease to, that nothing of the sort has happened in quite a while. . . . That's all I can say about it. Well, I guess up there it's arbitrary. Or maybe there are too many of us, and now it's someone else's turn. . . . I think simply when it happens you hear it. You can't really deny it. You try to be as rational as you can be, but, well, it doesn't work. In fact, I think one of the prerequisites for that is—well, it normally arrives when you are indeed at the end of your rope.[6]

You don't have one of these experiences and forget it anytime soon.

Joseph was a man who had a very strong sense of sacredness, of being, the sacredness of language, of poetry, and of human existence; but I think he somewhere said that you don't have to go to a church, you don't have to read certain books in order to have contact with God. He used the word "God" a lot, you know.

He did, didn't he?

---

5 When he was twenty-three, he was arrested, imprisoned, held at a psychiatric hospital, put on trial, and exiled to the Arctic Circle.

6 These events were described in Missy Daniel's 1990 *Threepenny Review* interview, in Haven, *Joseph Brodsky: Conversations*, 124–25.

He used it the first time he said goodbye to me, he said, you know, "God keep you or God preserve you," "Khrani Vas Bog, Dzhordzh."

By this time he spoke some English, but I take it that English was not the language of these early conversations.

He began to study English as a teenager, and by 1972, it was very serviceable. But he didn't become fluent until he was in his late twenties.

I would say later than that. His English lapsed into incomprehensibility for years after his arrival in the United States.

Perhaps spoken. But his sense of literary English was so keen and subtle that his criticisms and suggestions directed at my draft translations were penetrating and helpful. Always.

But I take it that these early meetings, nevertheless, were not *in English.*

Fortunately, I had become fluent in Russian by my late twenties, and that was years before this meeting. During our conversations in 1967 and 1968, we spoke Russian. Since about 1974, we have sometimes used English. His letters to me were usually in Russian, sprinkled with English words and phrases. Mine were usually in English, with a parallel sprinkling of Russian words and phrases.

The conversations continued in 1968, when you returned in June. Anything memorable you'd like to share?

The White Nights. Brodsky rented a rowboat and took two or three of us up and down the Neva or Fontanka at 1:00 a.m., an hour when one could still easily read the newspaper *Pravda*.[7]

---

7   According to Kline's datebook, this magical evening would appear to have happened on Saturday, June 22. He has a notation of a 7:00 p.m. appointment with Joseph and "Chertkov"—presumably his friend Leonid Chertkov in Leningrad. Joseph would write a poem for Chertkov's birthday on December 14, 1969: "Liubov' k Leonidu Chertkovu / est' nasha forma bytiia. . . ." This poem is published in Tat'iana Nikol'skaia, *Avangard i okrestnosti* (Sankt-Peterburg: Izd-vo Ivana Limbakha, 2002), 298. Chertkov, a poet himself, died in Germany in 2000.

On one of these early visits, he offered you the book of poetry he had been given by Akhamatova.

With the words "Iosifu Brodskomu, ch'i stikhi kazhutsia mne volsheb-nymi"—"To Joseph Brodsky, whose poems seem magical to me," and signed Moscow, 28 December 1963. He called it a "tsarstvennyi podarok"—that is, a gift fit for a king.

In a 1956 poem "Son (A dream)," she had used the expression "tsarst-vennyi podarok," possibly referring to a gift Sir Isaiah Berlin had brought her from England.

Of course, I thanked him profusely, but insisted I couldn't accept such a gift. I had second thoughts later. The book appeared to have been lost on Brodsky's emigration. But he had given it to Baryshnikov, who in turn donated it to the Akhmatova Museum in St. Petersburg, where it is now safely ensconced.

Short and Long Poems

Let's discuss that 1965 book Stikhotvoreniia i poemy *[Short and long poems] a little. It was published via smuggled manuscript that had been gathered by Konstantin Kuzminsky and Grigory Kovalev.*

Gleb Struve and Boris Filipoff were the co-editors in the United States. They had already edited several important editions of Russian poetry in the West, including works of Akhmatova and Mandelstam, among others. This new book was 239 pages, distilled from samizdat sources, published by the Inter-Language Literary Associates of Washington and New York. They did their best with the manuscripts that were available to them in 1964. Then they omitted their names from the title page to protect Brodsky, and Struve adopted the nom de plume "Georgii Stukov" for his introductory essay.

I understand Brodsky had mixed feelings about the results.

Brodsky saw the first copy of the book after he returned from internal exile in Norenskaya. Obviously, he was pleased to see an émigré volume of his poems—he was twenty-five at the time, and virtually unpublished in his own country.

But he'd changed a lot as a poet between 1957 and 1965, the time covered in *Stikhotvoreniia i poemy.*

He'd written "Gorbunov and Gorchakov" about his time in a psychiatric hospital. And "Verses on T. S. Eliot," while in Norenskaya. Certainly his experiences had matured him as a poet and as a human being.

Well, that's why he was unhappy. He was disappointed that the book included so much juvenilia. He was also annoyed by misprints and minor errors, though I suspect that he realized the difficulty when the editors are working with *samizdat* manuscripts, with no opportunity to consult the author.

For the collection I suggested, which would become *Ostanovka v pustyne* [A halt in the desert], he quickly typed up a list of twenty-six poems from 1957 to 1961 that he did *not* want included. Of the twenty-six, twenty-two had in fact been included in the 1965 volume—"Fish in Winter," "The Gladiators," and "The Pushkin Monument," among them.

Later, in 1992, when the first two volumes of *Sochineniia Iosifa Brodskogo* [The works of Joseph Brodsky] appeared in St. Petersburg, only fourteen of those twenty-six poems were omitted, and twelve were still included. The survivors included "The Jewish Cemetery near Leningrad," "The Pilgrims," and "I, like Ulysses."

Of course, the Russian writer Vladimir Maramzin had attempted to create a complete samizdat edition of Brodsky's poems, including painstaking search for dates and scholarly commentary. Joseph had corrected the text, about 2,000 pages. Mikhail Kheifets wrote an introductory essay for it. In 1974, both were arrested, their homes searched, and manuscripts confiscated. Both were sent to labor camps.[8]

That's right.

I think he was a bit hard on some of these early poems I've heard before about his disapproval of his "juvenilia." They're part of his history, and I, for one, very much like some of those poems that he slighted—and certainly the

---

8   Both were accused of anti-Soviet propaganda and agitation and tried by the Leningrad City Court. Maramzin was sentenced to five years in a labor camp, although the sentence was commuted in July 1975 and he was allowed to emigrate. Kheifets served four years in a labor camp and two years in internal exile.

Russian people did. They quoted them and memorized them. Why did he relent, do you think?

He may have wanted to cut them, but the editors in St. Petersburg may have reminded him that Maramzin and Kheifets had been brutally punished for compiling the four-volume samizdat collection of his poems in 1972. That served as the basis for the edition of 1992–95.

Meanwhile, other events were happening far away: in 1967, the year that you met the poet, Lord Nicholas Bethell published Joseph Brodsky: Elegy to John Donne and Other Poems, *with Longmans in London—Joseph's first publication in English. He was completely unaware of it. Hard to believe such a thing could happen, but . . . it was another era.*

A curious coda: On October 13, 1968, Joseph received a letter from Bethell telling him about his translation of the poems in the volume and congratulating him with the first English-language publication. Joseph wasn't pleased with the translation, which was put together without his knowledge or participation, and he disavowed it.

A Halt in the Desert

So the original plan was to publish a Russian-language volume of his poems Ostanovka v pustyne, *or* A Halt in the Desert, *as the title poem is called in English. The publisher was to be Inter-Language Literary Associates?*

In 1967, we learned that several supposedly "independent" cultural organizations were in fact subsidized by the CIA. They included not only the Congress for Cultural Freedom, the journal *Encounter (Встреча)*, but also the Inter-Language Literary Associates. None of these organizations had an intelligence function; all were engaged promoting cultural and intellectual freedom, which included the publishing of literary works then banned in the Soviet Union—the poetry of Akhmatova, Mandelstam, and Brodsky.

Because of the scandal, however, the publishing house had to halt its publishing program. So you're right. For awhile in the late 1960s, it was unclear who would publish *Ostanovka v pustyne*, as Brodsky had decided to call the new book, and how the publication would be supported.

Did these publication efforts make the Soviet authorities nervous?

They did. Filipoff and I were alarmed by a report in the Polish émigré journal *Kultura*, based in Paris, that Joseph had been arrested on the 10th of December, 1967. This was an exaggeration. Joseph had only been interrogated, something that happened to him more than once during this period.

Moreover, he'd published two of his important 1965 poems in a 1967 Leningrad almanac, *Den' poezii* [Day of poetry], which did not calm them—"Verses on the Death of T. S. Eliot" and "In Villages God Does Not Live in Corners."

Joseph Brodsky in Leningrad, 1972. (Photo: Lev Poliakov)

That must have thrown a monkey wrench into your plans for publication.

Filipoff wrote me on the 18th of December, telling me about the harsh campaign that authorities were waging against authors who were publishing abroad. Sinyavsky, whose pen name was Abram Tertz, was the particular troubling example. Filipoff suggested delaying the new publications for several months. I agreed. In my letter to him on the 28th, I suggested that it would be "embarrassing and perhaps dangerous for Brodsky to have the second edition appear now." I suggested we delay for half a year.

But things hadn't changed much six months later. On May 18, 1968, Filipoff wrote me again—I'm translating from the Russian: "And now the question arises: how and when should we publish [Brodsky's] book of longer and shorter poems? Would that not harm him, now that they have begun to publish him over there? Without your advice I don't want even to raise the question of bringing out a new, enlarged and revised collection."

However, Joseph had different ideas.

When I saw him the following month, in June, he was quite willing to meet me on several occasions—always a risk. He also insisted that whatever the Soviet authorities might say or do, he still wanted to have both the Russian-language *A Halt in the Desert* and a volume of new English translations published abroad.

Boris Filipoff and I decided early on that there would be no introductory essay to *A Halt in the Desert*. We wanted to let the poems speak for themselves. Again, Joseph had other ideas. He had introduced me to his friend Anatoly Naiman in 1967, and we'd become friendly. He'd written a short essay on Joseph's poetry in 1965—*Zametki dlia pamiati* [Notes for memory]. Both of them thought it would make a suitable foreword.

I recall vividly how Tolia was typing away furiously on Joseph's old Cyrillic portable typewriter on the afternoon of June 17,[9] as a taxi waited at the curb to take me to the airport for a 6:00 p.m. flight to Kiev. That manuscript was among several that I smuggled out of the country on that occasion.

Tolia made it very clear that his name couldn't be on the final product. He reiterated that in a message conveyed through Amanda Haight, who had met Tolia and Joseph in the 1960s and later published a short biography of Akhmatova—"the foreword, if you use it, *must* be anonymous," she had written from London on October 18, 1969.

So in the final book, the essay was signed simply "N N," which is the Russian version of "author anonymous."

---

9   My reading of Kline's datebooks suggests that he left for Kiev on June 27, not June 17.—
    C. L. H.

So how was the matter of publication resolved?

Some time in 1967 I had met Edward Kline, through our mutual friends Max Hayward and Boris Filipoff. No relation, although he quickly became a friend. The New York businessman had actively taken on the cause of Soviet dissidents, and was a personal friend of Andrei Sakharov and Elena Bonner, Valery Chalidze, and Pavel Litvinov. He was also the president of the revived Chekhov Publishing Co. [Izdatel'stvo imeni Chekhova]. Financial support came from Kline Brothers Company, from the publisher William Jovanovich, and later from the Ford Foundation.

Max Hayward was its general editor, with an office at Columbia University. The original incarnation of Chekhov Publishing had put out volumes of Khomiakov, Vladimir Solovyov, Rozanov, Zoshchenko and Akhmatova. The revived house published Nadezhda Mandelstam's memoirs—its greatest achievement. But certainly another landmark was publishing *Ostanovka v pustyne* [A halt in the desert] in May 1970.

Ostanovka v pustyne was the first book over which Brodsky had editorial control. The 1970 volume was inclusive of the one five years earlier, for the most part. Brodsky insisted we finally drop those twenty-two poems from the earlier book, which had been included against his wishes, and add nearly thirty he'd written during the period in between.

Things were heating up in the Anglophone world by then. A potential rival edition to Ostanovka v pustyne *came on the scene at some point. Tell me a little about that.*

That happened in September 1968. Lord Nicholas Bethell and Vladimir Czugunow, or in Russian Chugunov, announced their plans to publish a collection. They claimed to have known nothing about our plans, and had been reluctant to cancel their own without written assurances that an American edition was imminent.

I wrote to Faith Wigzell, a friend of Joseph's and a professor at the University of London, and explained to her that a written document could be dangerous to Joseph if the KGB got wind of it. That was the following January 3, 1969.

In the end, Bethell and Czugunow accepted the assurances of Max Hayward when he spoke with them in England in May 1969 and told him that our edition of of *Ostanovka v pustyne* was indeed imminent. The rival edition was abandoned.

In fact, *A Halt in the Desert* might well have appeared in 1969, except that Max Hayward and I were still holding on so that we could include Joseph's remarkable 1,400-line poem "Gorbunov and Gorchakov." Joseph definitely wanted it and it certainly deserved to be included. As you recall, he later referred to it as his "dar russkomu iazyku"—his gift to the Russian language.

Joseph completed it in late 1968, and it didn't reach us till the middle of the following year. It arrived via the diplomatic pouch, dispatched from Moscow by Carl Proffer, a professor of literature at the University of Michigan. He also had been a friend of Brodsky's since the 1960s. He co-founded, with his wife Ellendea, the *Russian Literature Triquarterly*, and also Ardis, the publishing house the would publish Brodsky in Russian—*Chast' rechi* [A part of speech] in 1977 and his *Konets prekrasnoi epokhi* [The end of the belle époque], which was edited by Lev Loseff and Vladimir Maramzin. By the time Carl had gotten that long poem to Washington via diplomatic pouch, and then to New York, publication had been delayed until early 1970.

Eventually, *A Halt in the Desert*—or *Ostanovka v pustyne*—carried only the name of Max Hayward as general editor. Although Max and Kline considered me to be the book's editor, we all thought it would be best if my name didn't appear in the book, after my 1968 KGB interrogation. I was clearly on their blacklist, and it would only hurt Brodsky.

In any case, Joseph was the real editor—he chose the poems and ordered them, as well as supplying the titles for the six numbered sections of the book: *Kholmy* [The hills], *Anno Domini, Fontan* [The fountain], *Ostanovka v pustyne, Gorbunov i Gorchakov,* and *Perevody* [Translations].

Amanda Haight saw Brodsky and Naiman in Moscow in September 1970, and wrote me in late December to say that the manuscript "seems to be greeted generally with great approval" and that Joseph was "definitely thrilled with it." Not so thrilled, however, that he didn't immediately enter corrections of misprints and minor errors in the copy that Amanda had taken to Naiman.

Later he sent me the list of corrections, too late. They were used much later to prepare Ardis's reprint of the book in 1988.

The Penguin Edition of *Joseph Brodsky: Selected Poems*

I remember my introduction to Joseph Brodsky's poems: the pale green image of the poet highlighted in purple on the cover of the Penguin Selected Poems— *the style sounds like typical 1970s garishness, but it was striking and memorable and oddly pleasing. It was a terrific collection, and introduced Brodsky to a wide audience in the West. How did it come about?*

Both Amanda and Faith knew Nikos Stangos, the new editor at Penguin Books in London. He was in charge of the series on Modern European Poets. He had "inherited," so to speak, a contract to publish an enlarged, and presumably revised, version of Lord Bethell's *Elegy to John Donne and Other Poems.*

Faith told me that she supplied the photo that is on the cover, though the photo is not green, of course! Joseph had given her the black and white photo. But tell me more about the genesis of this important volume.

In June 1968, even before *Ostanovka v pustyne* was published, Stangos got in touch with Amanda, who showed him my 1965 translation of "Elegy for John Donne" and a few other poems. So Stangos wrote me on July 10, inviting me to do the Penguin Brodsky. He agreed with Brodsky and me— at least as conveyed by Amanda—that the Bethell translations were "hasty, inaccurate, and awkward." He was ready to break the contract with Bethell and his publisher Longmans and offer me a contract for an entirely new set of translations.

At first Bethell resisted. As Faith Wigzell, who was acting as an intermediary, had written me on August 2, they had "a dragon of an agent"— literary agent, that is. But by November, Bethell and Longmans had been persuaded to give up their contract with Penguin. I signed the new contract on December 10. But at that point, I'd only finished a fraction of the translations that would be needed for the books, which would eventually have 168 pages by the time it was published in 1973. I finished the rest over the next four years. Many were published in literary journals and revised before they were included in the book.

Penguin was a big coup for someone who was, really, a little-known poet in the West, and presumably represented some financial risk. Eventually, W. H. Auden became involved too. How did that happen?

Arcady Nebolsine and Yury Ivask, both professors of Russian literature, knew Auden. They'd encouraged his interest in Russian thought and culture—so did the émigré doctor and author Vasily Yanovsky, who had at one time been Auden's personal physician. Auden wrote a foreword to Yanovsky's English-language novel *No Man's Time* in 1967 and was to review Ivask's two-volume edition of the works of Konstantin Leontyev in the *New Yorker* in April 1970.

So Nebolsine introduced me to Auden, and I visited him several times at his apartment in New York.

And then, the connection with Joseph Brodsky . . .

In brief, when, in Leningrad in 1968, I asked Brodsky who he would like to have write the foreword to *Selected Poems*. He replied unhesitatingly, "Auden, of course. But I doubt that he would do it."

I had given Auden a number of my Brodsky translations and introductory notes and essays on Brodsky's poetry. By May 1969, he had agreed to write the foreword for the Penguin book.

In December 1969, he wrote from New York to acknowledge that he'd gotten about a hundred printed pages of translations, but that he'd have to see my introduction before he could write his foreword.

In fact, he had completed the foreword by April 23, 1970, having, as I recall, only seen an early draft of the introduction.

Brodsky must have been thrilled.

I wanted to send it to Joseph, however circuitous the route. So I immediately had the text of Auden's foreword, which came to about six pages in normal typescript, retyped single-spaced throughout, with narrow margins, so that it would fit on two onionskin pages.

As it happened, my friend Michael Curran was leaving for Leningrad at the end of April. He had already met Brodsky when he was an exchange student at Leningrad University in 1966. He volunteered to hand-carry the foreword. He entered the Soviet Union by train from Helsinki. Knowing that the border guards there were especially tough, he decided en route to take the two folded sheets out of his inner pocket and slip them under the slightly loose bottom of the canvas bag. It turned out to be a brilliant move: he was given a thorough body search, which would certainly have turned up the smuggled document if it had been in his pocket or wallet. The guard in fact slipped his fingers into the loose bottom of the canvas bag, but didn't reach quite far enough to find the tiny square of folded paper.

He delivered the document to Joseph early in May. Naturally, Joseph greeted it with a mixture of astonishment, delight, and gratitude. He even ventured to write to Auden—through open mail, I believe—to thank him.

And so your friendship with Auden continued.

Auden invited me to visit him at Kirchstetten on July 21, 1970, where he later met Brodsky in June 1972. By then, Auden had written the foreword and Curran, a historian of Russia at Ohio State University, had taken it to Joseph in Leningrad.

We had a pleasant and productive visit. I read him the revised text of my introduction. In a letter I wrote to Stangos the next day, from Paris, I wrote that he had assured me that he found it "just about right," saying "what needed to be said about Brodsky as a poet."

Things were not going smoothly with the Penguin edition elsewhere.

You're right. On July 28, 1969, Stangos dropped an unrelated bombshell. Al Alvarez, who was the poetry consultant to Penguin Books, had offered me some helpful advice for improving my draft translations. Together, however, they decided it would be good to include about fifty pages of the poet Natalya Gorbanevskaya in the Brodsky volume. She and Joseph were friends—later, she would even be in a small group he invited to the Nobel ceremonies in Stockholm.[10]

But this was in 1969, and at that time she was mostly known as a political dissident and activist. She had boldly condemned the Soviet-led

---

10 In fact, Gorbanevskaya was never invited to the ceremony; she attended as a correspondent of the Paris newspaper, *Russkaia mysl'* (Polukhina, *Brodsky through the Eyes of His Contemporaries*, 1:260).

invasion of Czechoslovakia in August 1968 and had suffered at the hands of the secret police.

She was arrested in December of that year, and the following year sent to a psychiatric hospital.

My response to Stangos was adamant. Here's what I wrote on August 10: "It is vitally important that Brodsky be presented as a poet, not as a political dissident or agitator. Therefore his work must *not* be associated with that of anyone known primarily for political dissent and agitation." I said that she was unquestionably a woman of integrity and courage, but she might "reasonably be called a 'civic poet'; but that epithet does not apply to Brodsky—any more than it would apply to Donne or Eliot, despite the fact that all three are concerned, as men, poets, and citizens, about freedom."

Gorbanevskaya's poetry, at least what I've read of it, is lyrical and personal, but I can certainly understand why you might want to take that line with Stangos.

Stangos asked what Brodsky thought. I responded: "As for asking Brodsky's opinion of this matter, I'm sure he would react as I have. But I would, frankly, consider it too dangerous to try to raise the question with him, however indirectly." I added, "Forgive me if I seem overly vehement; but this may be literally a matter of life or freedom for Iosif Brodsky, a superb poet, and a human being whom I dearly love and respect." I was relieved when Stangos agreed later that month to drop the idea.

Meanwhile, your contact with Joseph in Leningrad continued.

From my departure from the USSR to the time of his exile, we continued to exchange New Year's and birthday cards, letters, and cablegrams.

But the serious communications about texts and translations happened via courier, yes?

Right, and it was frustratingly slow. Messages were hand-carried by visitors, including Faith, Amanda, and Véronique Schiltz, a close friend who was professor of archaeology at the University of Besançon in France, and an expert on Scythian art. She had met Joseph in Leningrad in the mid-60s, and became one of the principal translators of his poetry and prose into French.

Can you tell me a little more about these furtive communications?

Sometimes I sent a list of questions which Brodsky would answer in a separate note—or else the courier would speak to him and write back. In other cases he jotted down his answers, often in red ink, on the typed sheet with my questions and gave this to the visitor to bring back to London or Paris or New York.

In yet other cases, he would copy out answers to my questions into the notebook of a visitor, sometimes with new poetic texts. For example, Kathryn Gibson, a graduate student from Columbia University was the courier in August 1969. She came back with neatly handwritten texts for three splendid new poems: "Pochti elegiia" [Almost an elegy], written in fall 1968; "Zimnim vecherom v Ialte" [A winter evening in Yalta], from January 1969; and "Stikhi v Aprele" [Verses in April], from spring 1969.

In November of 1970, Joseph sent me a list of corrections for *Ostanovka v pustyne*. Véronique Schiltz brought me a photocopy of the corrections he had made in Leningrad, inserting it in her copy of *Stikhotvoreniia i poemy*. This helped not only with *Ostanovka v pustyne*, but also the translations of certain poems in both Russian volumes, since some of the corrections involved changes of meaning.

Isaiah Berlin wrote you from Wolfson College, Oxford, on 14 January, 1970, to say, "He seems to me the most moving poet now alive, even if he is not the best, and I am happy to have anything by him and happy to have your translations." That qualification, "even if he is not the best," would have rankled his friend Akhmatova.

Later, on 11 May, 1970, he wrote to ask how he could send a cable to Joseph, and worried "such a cable from someone like me would compromise him therefore ultimately do more harm than good, whatever pleasure he might experience." "I admire his verse very much indeed as you may imagine. But I do not know what kind of list I am on with the Soviet authorities, and I would hate to think that anything I did would make his position heavier to bear. Shall I get Lowell to send him something."

You suggested it might be more prudent for someone like Lowell to send the greetings, since "you may be on some high-level Soviet black list." The greetings must have meant a lot, since Berlin had hosted Akhmatova's visit to London and Oxford in 1965.

Meanwhile, the back-and-forth with Penguin in London, in addition to surreptitious communication with Leningrad, continued. Even as it became clearer to everyone that Joseph Brodsky could not stay in the USSR.

Stangos and Alvarez communicated with me on editorial and translation issues by letter, sometimes by cablegram, and in one or two cases by telephone between London and Ardmore, Pennsylvania. We met twice, in August 1968 and July 1970, in Stangos's London office.

Brodsky met with Stangos in that office, with Alvarez and Auden, after he left the Soviet Union in June 1972. By the time he returned in June 1973, the *Selected* was already in production.

The Auden endorsement certainly helped Joseph, but more importantly, the connection evoked Auden's considerable paternal instincts. He sponsored Joseph's astonishing debut at London's Poetry International Festival in June 1972, which I wrote about in The Kenyon Review:

> When the disheveled, nervous, and unknown poet walked to the podium, time seemed to stop. "It was an astonishing and, at the same time, almost tragic performance. That is, there were tragic dimensions to it—a young poet, virtually alone on stage," recalled Daniel Weissbort, who had also attended London's Poetry International Festival in June 1972.
>
> Joseph Brodsky had been expelled from the Soviet Union only a few days earlier, and W. H. Auden had taken him under his broad, protective wing, shielding him from journalists as best he could. Weissbort recalled that the younger poet was "alone in the world, with nothing but his poems, nothing but the Russian language, of which he was already a 'master,' or as he would have preferred to say, 'a servant.'"
>
> Then the poet poured out his poems in the hypnotic incantation that was to become his trademark: an archaic sound—a lament from a lost civilization, an ancient prayer, or simply a metronomic wail. And then it was over.
>
> "When he ended, the audience was as stunned as the poet on stage was now silent—inaccessible, emptied, a kind of simulacrum of himself. It was as if

the air had been drained of sound. And the appropriate response would have been that, a soundlessness, in which you would hear only your own breathing, be aware only of your own physicality, your isolated self," says Weissbort, who later became one of Brodsky's translators. "To say we were impressed is putting it far too mildly. We were moved, emotionally, even physically."[11]

---

11 Cynthia L. Haven, "Uncle Grisha Was Right," *Kenyon Review* 28, no. 3 (Spring 2006): 159–68.

Chapter 3

Did the KGB Defend Russian Poetry?

A backdrop to Joseph Brodsky's Leningrad life was surveillance, wiretapped conversations, smuggled manuscripts. During the Cold War era, our idea of the KGB in the Eastern bloc was certainly shaped by James Bond movies, Mission: Impossible, *and other fantasies. Your KGB interrogations had a sinister side, but also a comic one, and there seems to have been as much incompetence as calculation.*

I've been thinking about some of the strange aspects of my encounters with the KGB. We need to explore that question further, because my two major encounters had to do with Joseph.

As an American citizen, what could they do to you except throw you out of the USSR and deny you future visas?

Yes, they could certainly do all of those things. But they could do much more. Only a few years earlier, in 1963, Fred Barghoorn, a Yale professor who specialized in Soviet politics, was crudely framed, arrested, and held in the infamous Lubyanka prison for a total of sixteen days, spending much of that time in solitary confinement. While walking on a Moscow street, Barghoorn was approached by a stranger who shoved a roll of documents into his hands. He was instantly handcuffed and led away to be charged with espionage on the basis of his "having had classified Soviet documents in his possession." I was acutely aware of this incident, because Ellen Mickiewicz, Barghoorn's former graduate student, who had worked tirelessly for his release, was a friend of mine. The Soviet authorities, with awkward irony, underlined Barghoorn's predicament by offering him as reading matter a Russian translation of Dreiser's *An American Tragedy*.[1]

When did the KGB become interested in you? Was it in 1968?

It started long before that, long before I met Brodsky, although eventually some of those earlier encounters became woven into his story. As far as I know, I was not trailed on my first visit to Russia in 1956, but I definitely was in 1957, and from then onwards to 1968. In a word, I was trailed on five of my six visits over a thirteen-year period. Bear in mind that in the fall of 1956 the Hungarian uprising was brutally crushed by the Soviet military.[2] In the following year, the cultural and intellectual atmosphere in Leningrad, Moscow, and Kiev was much worse. There was definitely less freedom, tighter control of thought and expression, and more anxiety among the Russians I met in 1957 than there had been in 1956.

In 1960, I spent the longest time in one visit to the Soviet Union that I ever spent—a total of six weeks. Friends of mine, such as the Russian scholar Jim Scanlan, who were doing similar work, were able to spend a semester or even a year in the USSR. I tried to do the same in the academic year 1964–65, and was accepted by the American side, but after long delays the Soviets turned me down.

To be clear, according to your datebook from that year, you were in the Soviet Union from July 3 to August 14, followed by your first visit to Poland on September 14–18. Then you traveled to Prague and Budapest, among other

---

1   In what would be his last press conference, President John Kennedy denounced the action as "unjustified" and "a very serious matter." The professor was eventually expelled, calling his detention "inexplicable and mysterious." Because of the incident, the United States called off negotiations for cultural exchanges. Bruce Lambert, "Frederick Barghoorn, 80, Scholar Detained in Soviet Union in 1963," *New York Times*, November 26, 1991.

2   On October 23, 1956, thousands of Hungarians took to the streets to demand democratic reforms and freedom from Soviet oppressions. Soviet tanks rolled in on November 4 and crushed the revolt within a week. It is estimated that about 2,500 Hungarians were killed and 200,000–250,000 fled. It was the first major threat to Soviet power, and the clampdown horrified the West.

places. So tell me about your first confrontations with the KGB. Did you ever confront the KGB agents who were following you that year?

Yes, as it happened. Twice on the same day in 1960, with two different agents. As I left my Moscow hotel, I noticed that someone was following me. I tested him by stopping, going back, and buying a newspaper, and he stopped and went back and pretended to buy something.

My cotton socks, after almost two months on the road, had developed several holes. So I did what any American would do in London or Paris: I asked the chambermaid if she would please mend them for me and offered her a couple of bucks in the local currency. The Russian chambermaid's answer surprised me. She said, "No, no, I can't do that. We have specialists for that."

Specialists for mending socks?

Yes, specialists who worked at a special place a few blocks from my hotel. The place didn't have a name, only a street number. You went down a few steps and opened a door. And you saw two long lines of women. In one line were women with shopping bags full of silk stockings with runs that they needed to have mended. In the other line were the women who had returned a week later to pick up their mended stockings. The reason the first line moved so slowly was that each woman had more than one pair of nylon stockings, and each stocking had at least one run. Every single run, even if there were a dozen of them, had to be carefully measured (was it twelve millimeters long, or only eight, or perhaps just six?) and priced at so many kopecks per millimeter. Then each woman was given a receipt with a date, at least a week later, when her mended stockings would be ready to pick up.

I was literally the only man in that large room, until my KGB tail opened the door and walked in. He looked somewhat confused, as though he had never been in that room before. That's when I turned to him and said in Russian, "Comrade, it's not worth the wait. The lines are too long and they move too slowly. I'd advise you to buy yourself some new socks." As I recall, he blushed slightly and quickly disappeared. Of course, after I'd confronted him, he had to be replaced. That was KGB policy.

Usually when I left my hotel room I stayed away for several hours, visiting people, sightseeing, or working in the library. But in this case, after picking up my mended socks, I returned in less than an hour to my hotel. The woman at the desk near the elevator, the *dezhurnaia*, whose job it is to take and file your room key with its heavy wooden handle when you leave, and give it to you when you return, pretended not to understand the room number I was asking for—though my Russian was perfectly adequate. I soon realized that she was stalling, while she frantically pushed some secret button or lever to alert the KGB agent who she knew was in my room at that very moment.

As it happened, the agent didn't have time to get away. When I opened my door, there he stood. I assume he had been searching my papers and had doubtless photographed certain pages. His "cover" was pretty thin, almost comical. He pretended to be waxing my floor. He had some kind of felt or woolen pad wrapped around his shoe and was tracing large circles on my hardwood floor. His verbal excuse was pretty thin, too. He said, in Russian, something like, "Sir, your floor really needed a good waxing." He certainly didn't look like a floor waxer or a manual laborer of any kind. He was wearing a neat jacket, a white shirt and tie, and looked rather like a busy young lawyer or accountant.

You once told me about other such "specialists" you needed on that same trip.

It turned out that I had driven my VW bug so many kilometers that I had to get an oil change. I asked the people at the filling station where I purchased my gasoline—using coupons I had pre-purchased with dollars—to please change the oil. They said, "No, no, we can't do that. You have a dirty car." I said, "Okay, well, please give me a car wash." And they said, "No, no, we can't do that. We've got specialists who do that. And they gave me the address of a car wash somewhere north of Leningrad."

Um, a specialist for a car wash?

Yes, a specialist for a car wash. And apparently it was while driving to the car wash that I had been tracked in the vicinity of a Soviet military installation, something I had no idea about at the time.

And then, on to Poland . . .

I met Leszek Kołakowski in Warsaw, during the summer of that year. I had previously met a Polish sociologist in this country—Adam Podgorecki.

He'd been in the United States on some sort of fellowship, and he spoke adequate English. In 1960, I looked him up in Warsaw. His former wife had invited him to her birthday party the next day in your favorite town—Kraków. I was planning to drive to Kraków on my way to Zakopane and Czechoslovakia and I offered him a ride. So we headed for Kraków.

We were alone in the car and we were speaking English and I assume—well, I *know* now—that my rented 1960 VW had been supplied at the Finnish-Soviet border with electronic recording and radio-locating equipment. Our Polish "escorts" were in a Warszawa, the Polish version of the Soviet Pobeda, the automobile with the door hinges sticking out. A sturdy, cheap car. I suppose it was fitted with a more powerful engine, so they could have driven circles around me if they had wanted to.

They followed us all the way to Kraków, a trip of about four hours. On the downhill my 1960 VW bug could hit seventy or seventy-five miles an hour. But even on the uphill, when I was slowing down to fifty or fifty-five, they never tried to overtake or pass me.

There were four people in the Warszawa, three men and a woman. I'm not quite sure why they included the woman, or what her function was. It didn't look as though she was supposed to be the seductress. She didn't look like a very effective Mata Hari; she was middle-aged and heavy-set.

Actually, the real Mata Hari was getting on a bit, and no skinny sylph, either.

Maybe that Polish woman was fluent in English. Anyway, when we stopped to eat, they stopped. It was clear that this Warszawa was our "tail." At a certain point, as we were getting closer to Kraków, Adam said, "See the side road just beyond that big tree on the right?" He added, "Go down there as fast as you can and abruptly turn right." After I turned right, he guided me through a few more turns to a spot fairly close to the hotel I was planning to stay at, the Orbis Hotel in Kraków. Adam jumped out at an open streetcar terminal. He knew the city well, having lived there for several years, and he had directed me to a place where he could quickly climb onto a streetcar and disappear.

I know that side of town. I had an apartment right around the corner.

You know that side of town, then. Adam and I made a little arrangement. I would phone him at his ex-wife's number. If, in response, Adam used a certain expression, that meant that he had not been picked up and interrogated. When he actually used that expression, I felt greatly relieved. After I dropped Adam off, I went to the Orbis Hotel where I thought I had a reservation. It turned out that there had been some sort of bureaucratic mix-up, and I had to go to a different hotel. It took at least fifteen minutes to straighten things out. And when I emerged from the hotel, the Warszawa was parked on the other side of the street, a discreet two blocks away. So they obviously didn't let me out of their sight for very long. They had followed my every move on their radio locator.

Amazing that they had this kind of technology in 1960, so long before the public did!

Yes. In that respect the security services behind the Iron Curtain were "thoroughly modern." I didn't stay in Kraków long. I went up from there to Zakopane, a small town in the Tatra Mountains, fairly close to the Czech border. There I had my second meeting with Leszek Kołakowski, who was attending some kind of a weekend youth gathering.

Later, Adam Podgorecki's work in sociology became well known and highly respected. He died a few years ago. I kept in touch with his widow until recently. He spent most of his career in Canada and she still lives there.

So they asked you about this incident years later, in Leningrad?

Yes. They obviously were in touch with the secret police in Poland and had received a full report about where I had gone and which people I was seeing in Warsaw and Kraków.

But the KGB never brought you in for questioning during that long 1960 sojourn?

No. And there were so many things that they could've asked me when, in 1968, they finally did interrogate me. Why didn't they ask me, "What were you doing with that guy on the drive from Warsaw to Kraków? And why wasn't he still with you when you arrived in Kraków?"

Not only on this trip did they fail to interrogate you, but they also didn't question you on your trips in 1966 and 1967.

In the 1968 interrogation they admitted that they had been watching me closely in 1966, but that they didn't interrogate me then because of my daughter's serious illness, which caused us to leave Russia after only three weeks of a planned four-week stay.

More recently, I've been wondering why the KGB didn't interrogate me in 1967. They obviously knew that I was seeing Joseph. They kept him under constant surveillance. We used to take all the standard precautions. He would either have loud music playing and we would speak very softly to each other, or we would just write notes and pass them back and forth, so we couldn't be recorded. The KGB probably suspected that Joseph was, or would be, giving me unpublished poems to take out and publish and or translate.

Which he did. Under the circumstances it was rather courageous. You were unflinching. Soon afterwards you smuggled some of Brodsky's poems for the future collection, Ostanovka v pustyne [A halt in the desert], *out of the Soviet Union. You also gave Joseph some hard-earned money, which must have helped a lot in his stringent circumstances.*

Yes. In June 1968. I had given Joseph 250 roubles—nearly $300 in the exchange rate at the time for royalties for *Stikhotvoreniia i poemy* [Short and long poems]. Our last meeting was on the 27th.

By that time, we were already discussing a new émigré edition of his poems, and drafting a table of contents for both volumes. He gave me the manuscripts for several dozen new poems that hadn't been included in *Stikhotvoreniia i poemy*. I was searched at the border, but fortunately, they didn't find these poems inside my jacket pockets. I confess I was quaking in my boots.

I'll bet you were.

The jacket I was wearing had two deep inside pockets, and both pockets were absolutely crammed with Brodsky typescripts on A4 paper folded into quarters. There must have been a total of twenty-five or thirty of them. Of course, I was terrified that the border police were going to do a body search. At the Moscow airport, where I was about to board a flight to Amsterdam, they did a very careful, exhaustive search of my briefcase and my two suitcases. But fortunately, they didn't do a body search.

Joseph's longest poem, "Gorbunov and Gorchakov," which ran over forty pages in *Ostanovka v pustyne*, must have covered close to fifty type-script pages—much too long to fit into my jacket pockets. In 1968–69, there wasn't even a United States consulate in Leningrad. So Carl Proffer managed to carry the typescript from Leningrad to Moscow and send it from the Embassy there by diplomatic pouch.

So you got out with the poems. That took some guts after your run-in with the authorities. Let's go back and talk about your KGB interrogation.

Yes, on my same sixth visit to Russia in 1968. That's when the KGB finally confronted me. I have an exact date somewhere, but it was my first or second day in Leningrad. I believe on that trip we started in Moscow. In late August, I was staying in a Leningrad hotel.[3]

I was leading a fairly big group, a plane-full of people. This group was sponsored by the Citizens Exchange Corps, a volunteer group that had a good track record of putting people in touch with their professional counterparts in Russia. There were some students, but the group also included adults who were kindergarten teachers or firemen or truck-drivers—a cross-section of American society. So if American kindergarten teachers wanted to visit a Soviet kindergarten, the CEC could arrange that. Similarly with American firemen who wanted to visit a Soviet firehouse.

There were always problems with the Soviet bureaucracy, and I'd been dealing with the quite unpleasant assistant manager of the hotel. She came to me one day and announced, in a fairly unpleasant voice, "You need to see the director. He has some problems to discuss with you." I said, okay. She went up to a closed door and knocked. Apparently this was a private meeting room. She disappeared and two KGB agents approached me with their IDs held up, so I could see that they were with the Committee of State Security [Komitet gosudarstvennoi bezopasnosti]. That was the beginning of a two-hour-plus interrogation. The two agents told me their names, Vladimir and Nikolay, the two names that Lenin used—not their

---

3   My reading of George's datebook: On June 10 or 11, 1968, he flew to Russia, though it's not clear what city. He had meetings, apparently, with Joseph on June 22, 24, 25, and 27. He was in Kiev from 27 to 29, returning to Moscow on June 30 for a flight back to the US. George's notes are cryptic and hard to read, and it's entirely possible that unrecorded appointments and travels were added, but he died before I could question him more closely about the discrepancies.—C. L. H.

real names, of course. Both of them were professional-looking, in their late thirties or early forties.

Vladimir was senior and did most of the talking, and Nikolay was the linguist, the man who knew English, although we never used English that I recall. The whole interrogation was conducted in Russian. They made some very harsh initial charges—that in 1960 I had driven my VW north of Leningrad to the vicinity of a Soviet military installation, which of course I knew nothing about. As you recall, I was on my way to the place where I'd been told I could get my "dirty car" washed by specialists. I had the impression that when I said I knew nothing about being close to a military installation, they believed me.

In the last year or so, I've come to think that they used that opening charge as a kind of Potemkin village. In other words, they really had no suspicion at all that I was doing any military spying. But by delivering a harsh charge, they could sound tough.

Early in the interrogation, they said quite sternly, "And why were you trying to avoid our brotherly security services in the People's Republic of Poland?" Clearly, they had had access to the Polish secret police files from eight years before. And I remember what I said. "Mne prosto nadoelo"—"I was just fed up"—with being tailed, that is. And I was. That was true. But that was only part of the truth. The main reason was that I wanted to let Adam Podgorecki get away without the secret police picking him up and interrogating him.

They must have known that. Why didn't they ask, "Well, who was that Polish citizen with you?" If they wanted to be tough on me, why didn't they say, "We know you let somebody out." They didn't. They presumably had a transcript of our recorded conversation, so they didn't need to ask about that. In sum, as I realized only much later, they let me off pretty easily. And they didn't ask such questions later that month in 1968, when I was in Kiev, either.

However, I thought the two agents had been pretty hard on me. One thing that reinforced my impression was that they had, on a table beside them, two bound, loose-leaf notebooks. They looked like the draft of somebody's doctoral dissertation in history. Each notebook was at least two inches thick. Obviously that was the result of at least eleven years of their bugging me and bugging my phone conversations and following me on all six of my visits to the Soviet Union, except the first in 1956. Everything connected with my visits to the Soviet Union was in these two fat loose-leaf notebooks.

Of course, they never let me look at even a page of those notebooks, but they had various pieces of paper marking the pages they might want to refer to.

Now, you'll remember in 1966 my daughter Bunny became ill and we left Russia after three weeks. They said something about that: "Well, we've been keeping track of you, and we would have had this conversation in 1966, but your daughter got sick and we were being considerate." Looking back, I think it's possible that they really meant that.

But that doesn't explain why they didn't talk to me in 1967, the year I met Joseph. In 1966, I had had my third Moscow meeting with A. F. Losev, the elderly classical scholar and religious thinker who had spent three years in the Stalinist camps in the early 1930s. When I drove to his dacha near Moscow several KGB cars followed me and parked nearby. However, I don't recall either of the agents bringing up Losev's name, either.

Early in the 1968 interrogation Brodsky's name came up. The agents wanted to know what I discussed with Brodsky. Well, I told them we discussed poetry, and I remember at one point I mentioned the name Akhmatova. Their response, I suppose, was predictable. They made it very clear that for them she was "a hateful, odious figure." I remember the phrase "odioznaia figura." Of course they were thinking of her powerful poem "Requiem," which vividly depicts the brutality of the KGB during the great purges of the 1930s, in which her own son by Nikolay Gumilyov was a victim.

I didn't try to defend Akhmatova. But perhaps Vladimir already knew what I knew, namely, that Brodsky considered Akhmatova not just a great poet, but "the best human being he had ever met."

They also asked about a few other people in my group. One was a woman who had been born and raised in Russia but had lived in the States for a long time. As I recall, she taught Russian language and literature at Reed College, and had either just retired or was about to retire, and she wanted to see the place of her birth "one more time before she died." The KGB agents asked why she was so fluent in Russian and then why she wanted to come back to Russia.

In my group of about ninety, there were only two or three who were either native speakers or serious students of the Russian language. As I recall, Vladimir and Nikolay raised questions about all of them. But most of their questions were about my contacts and conversations with Brodsky. I vividly recall that, toward the end of the interrogation they made it abundantly clear that if I were going to return to the Soviet Union and meet with troublemakers or people unfriendly to the regime, such as Brodsky, "You will report your conversations with him to us." I vividly remember that phrase. It sounded like an order, certainly a directive that I would have no choice but to follow.

I also remember exactly what I said in reply, namely, "Ia mogu zhit′ bez Rossii"—"I can live without Russia." And I expected that I would have to do precisely that for the rest of my life. It was only because the Soviet Union left the world stage and Russia came back that I was able—in January 1991—to resume my long interrupted visits to Leningrad and Moscow. The occasion was the first international conference on Brodsky's life and work in Leningrad. I gave a paper in Russian on Russian-to-English and English-to-Russian translation. My main examples were my own translation of Brodsky's "Babochka" ("The butterfly") and Brodsky's splendid translation of Andrew Marvell's "Eyes and Tears." As you know, I went on to make a total of four more visits, the last in August 1993.

Let me make two final points about the KGB interrogations. First, toward the end of the first Leningrad interrogation, which lasted at least two hours, they came close to apologizing for having been so harsh at the beginning. Vladimir explained: "We have to be tough in the beginning. We don't know who you are and what your intentions are." I remember the phrase: "Ne znaia cheloveka"—"not knowing the person." Vladimir continued: "We had to speak harshly. We had to demand to know why you were in the vicinity of a Soviet military installation." The implication was that, at that point—this was perhaps an hour and a half into the interrogation—they had come to know me well enough to realize that I really wasn't a spy. But in the beginning they weren't sure and thought I might be. Now they were saying, in effect, "We now know you. You're just a professor, a decent guy, and not a spy. It's just that you're too close to people like Brodsky."

Second, they had said before they left me in Leningrad, "We will phone your hotel in Kiev"—where I would be staying the following week with my group. Of course they knew everything about my trip: my precise itinerary, which cities I'd be visiting, which hotels I'd be staying at, and when my visa would expire. I couldn't think of any reason why they would need to see me again, but in fact they did.

Why would they want to see me again? They'd asked me all the questions that I could answer about Brodsky and various members of my group. They had made it abundantly clear that if I ever came back to the Soviet Union and met with people like Brodsky I would be seeing them, reporting to them.

Not just seeing the KGB, but seeing those two men in particular? Is that what they meant?

That's a good question. I don't suppose they were the only agents assigned to me. I'm sure they weren't. Vladimir and Nikolay meant: you'll be seeing security officials, KGB agents.

But you did meet those same two KGB agents in Kiev.

Yes, the same agents. They were almost trying to be friendly, I guess you could say. They picked me up at my hotel and took me somewhere, a very pleasant room, and they had some excellent cognac. I forget whether there was anything to eat, there might have been. But this was in the evening, and they poured out cognac, and I remember the phrase: "Well, according to our half-established custom, let us . . ."—the implication was that we were now almost half-friends. I think they may have meant it in the sense that they had come to rather like me. Of course, they might just have been good actors and under the surface might still have distrusted or suspected me.

The obvious assumption would be that they were hoping to get more information out of you with cognac and conversation than they had with yelling and threats.

That may well have been their intention, but I can't recall any additional information they got out of me in Kiev. And there were so many things they could have asked, but again, as in Leningrad, didn't ask.

But in any case, they were less intimidating this time.

Frankly, I would say that the Kiev interrogation was not unpleasant, almost pleasant. I drank a little of their cognac, making sure I wouldn't get drunk. And at one point one of them, I think it was the younger one, said, "Well, you know, I'm married. I have an eleven-year-old daughter." He told me her name. And he went on with an almost lyrical account of her youth and innocence. She knew nothing about what her father did, and maybe that was just as well.

But now I wonder: Vladimir and Nikolay knew about my 1967 and 1968 meetings with Joseph in Leningrad, so why didn't they arrange for a body search when, shortly after the Kiev encounter, I was leaving the Moscow airport for Amsterdam? Is it possible they were really not doing their duty as KGB officers and were actually letting me leave the country with the manuscripts? I just don't know. I've talked to Jim Scanlan of Ohio State about this recently, and he doesn't know either.

You keep circling back to that, and it is *odd. Why* didn't *they confront you in 1967?*

Let me tell you what caused me to change my mind to make me think that somehow they were trying to protect me and protect Brodsky, especially Brodsky. I've come to that conclusion slowly and reluctantly. I certainly didn't think so in 1968.

In Kiev, which was a much less unpleasant encounter, they could have asked me, "Did Brodsky give you or offer you manuscripts to take out of the country to translate or publish?" They never asked me that question. I suppose if they had I would have had to tell them the truth. I don't know how it would have gone from there.

Instead, however, they mostly just asked you about your conversations?

Yeah, they wanted to know about our conversations.

So now, years later, you are coming to very different conclusions about these KGB interactions. What's the upshot?

A different conclusion is definitely emerging. In a way, I'm happy to reach it. In another way, I'm actually astonished to reach it. The emerging conclusion is that the KGB was really going easy on me. Not so much on me, as on Brodsky. They were deliberately permitting me to take the manuscripts out of the country. What I said earlier was true but incomplete, and thus misleading. I had said that probably the security wasn't quite so tight because I was leaving Leningrad for Kiev—in other words, I wasn't leaving the USSR.

Well, that was true of my departure from Leningrad, but in fact I flew back with my group from Kiev to Moscow and soon after that left the country from Moscow. And at the Moscow airport I was not body searched. As in Leningrad earlier, the border guards did a very thorough search of my briefcase and suitcases. But they didn't look in my jacket pockets and they didn't ask me to empty my pockets. They could have done either or both. Why didn't they? Now, of course, if I'm right and they really did deliberately refrain from ordering the border guards to do a body search, perhaps even ordering them to do an especially thorough search of my briefcase and suitcases instead, they were not going easy for my sake. They were doing it for the sake of a major Russian poet and, more broadly, for the sake of Russian literature.

That's an interesting supposition because it implies that the quality of Brodsky's work was known even to KGB agents. Certainly I wouldn't expect the American FBI to have such literary appreciation.

For example, in America, you wouldn't expect the border agents to know any American poet. You wouldn't expect the police to recognize Richard Wilbur. Or A.E. Stallings. Of course, she hasn't been a cause célèbre, but even if she had, I wouldn't expect people to have an opinion about her poetry.

I wouldn't have thought that the average KGB agent would be a connoisseur of poetry, certainly not enough of one to have an opinion about Joseph's poetry one way or the other. Now, you're suggesting that they did have an idea of his stature.

Yes, because the only other explanation is a level of sloppiness or incompetence that's hard to imagine either in the KGB or the border police.

That throws a whole new light on the trial in 1964, perhaps suggesting that when that trial happened, the people were not fooled about the goings-on and had some sense that a major poet was being put through a kangaroo trial.

Well, one has to make a distinction within the crowds that attended, or read about, the trial. Most of those in attendance were workers and peasants, who mouthed the official slogan "trial of a social parasite"—or *tuneiadets.* The few people who were witnesses for the defense and the many who read the newspaper accounts knew very well that Brodsky was a major Russian poet. His "Elegy for John Donne" dates from 1963, and by February–March

1964 had circulated fairly widely in samizdat. That was the text I saw in Warsaw in December 1964.

Right. I'm just saying that . . .

Don't forget that two important Brodsky poems, his "In Memory of T. S. Eliot," and the untitled short poem "In villages God does not live . . ." had been published in that big-circulation almanac *Den' poezii* in Leningrad in 1967. So he was not totally unpublished. His translations from the Spanish had been published in 1962 and others from the Serbo-Croatian in 1963.

But you make a very interesting point. I am indeed assuming that Vladimir and Nikolay knew about his poetry and knew that it was good.

So at his trial, the government had filled the hall with workers from local factories, who had never heard his name, let alone read his poetry.

Well yes, that's true, but don't forget that was in February and March 1964. We're talking now about August and September 1968.

Okay, okay. So that was true back in 1964.

Well, for one thing, samizdat was creating an audience for him. I saw the samizdat version of his "Elegy for John Donne" in Warsaw in December 1964.

Yes, that makes sense.

I'd like to add a couple of further points. The duty of Vladimir and Nikolay to the KGB and to the Soviet state required them to tell the Moscow border police that when Mr. Kline crosses the border, you should look in all of his pockets. He probably has something that he shouldn't be allowed to take with him. Why didn't they? I hadn't really puzzled about this until just over a year ago. I've been wondering, and I still don't have a definitive answer, but it seems increasingly likely that the Soviet authorities deliberately permitted me to leave the country with at least two dozen smuggled poems in my inside jacket pockets. The other possibility is that it was just a bureaucratic glitch. That could happen, but it doesn't seem very likely. What do you think?

It could just be sheer incompetence. In bureaucracies, a lot of things slip through the cracks. Look at our own national security. Even with twenty-first century technology, it still screws up. But who knows? You might be right.

Of course, I don't suppose anybody was thinking about a future Nobel laureate.

I did want to say one other thing. When they sneered at Akhmatova, I responded by asking, "Which poets do you favor?" And they gave me a name instantly. So they knew about poetry, and it was a poet I guess some people would say was fairly good. He gets into the anthologies and so on. His name is Robert Rozhdestvensky. Have you seen that name?

He was in the Voznesensky and Yevtushenko circle, wasn't he?

You can find some of his stuff in an anthology of Soviet poetry of the 1960s or 1970s. He was a poet favored by the nomenklatura, which may be an overgeneralization. But when you read some of his stuff, you realize that he was trying to be another Mayakovsky, glorifying Lenin in the 1920s at a time when Lenin was a godlike figure for Soviet readers.

Rozhdestvensky thought that communism would be around forever—at least until the thirtieth century. Lenin will be striding down the staircase of the ages, et cetera, et cetera. So I suppose these KGB agents may have had some feeling for poetry. Presumably they liked that political stuff and were happy in the thought that the Soviet state which they served would be around forever and be glorified by poets forever.

But what would you have said if they had asked you about smuggling poems out of the country?

I don't know what I would've said. But of course the truth would have been "Yes, I will have a lot of them."

Well, you had to lie. I mean, you can't just say yes.

I suppose I would have lied, but that surely wouldn't have prevented them from ordering a body search at the border. I've come to two fairly definite conclusions. Perhaps I should say one conclusion and the corollary to that conclusion. One is very positive about them, and one is very negative in terms of their duty. The conclusion is that they deliberately allowed Brodsky's poetry to leave the country, knowing that it would be published and translated abroad. The corollary is that by so doing they were betraying their organization and their country, to both of which they had sworn loyalty and allegiance.

Yes, assuming that they were supportive of the Soviet regime.

They were in a branch of the KGB that was different from others. Those harsh initial questions about my being in the vicinity of a military installation, I think they probably knew why I was there. And they knew that it had nothing to do with espionage. They were educated people. I assumed they had college degrees. And it's generally the case, almost universally the case, that an educated Russian knows and loves Russian poetry. It's something different from other cultures.

Yes, but that's something of a myth, surely?

I don't suppose there's any other culture where that's true, is there?

Poland.

Okay. Well, you know more about Poland than I do, but that's plausible, surely, yes, definitely.

So 1968 was your curious farewell to the KGB.

As I said, "Ia mogu zhit' bez Rossii." "I can live without Russia." I thought I'd live my whole life without Russia, and I did for more than twenty-two years. You realize, lots of people, lots of Americans, were going back and forth to and from the Soviet Union. But I never even applied for a visa until they announced the first international conference on the life and work of Joseph Brodsky in January of 1991 in Leningrad. It was still the Soviet Union, but it was high *glasnost*, and they were publishing all kinds of previously forbidden stuff—Solovyov, Berdyaev, Pasternak's *Dr. Zhivago*. It was pretty clear that the old Soviet system was crumbling, even though it didn't actually fall apart till December of that year.

And no sign of the KGB?

No evidence of the KGB anywhere. I was alert, but I'm sure that branch had been dissolved. In 1988, several of Brodsky's poems had been published in *Novyi mir*, which had a huge circulation, more than a million, just after the Nobel Prize. They also began publishing his work in the journal *Inostrannaia literatura* [Foreign literature] during the period 1986–1987, when glasnost really began, and December 1991, when it all ended.

I read a memoir in a Russian newspaper in the early 1990s by somebody who'd worked in a special branch of the KGB. I forget what the title of it was, but he said their main job was to prevent or break up contacts between foreign visitors like me and interesting Russians like Brodsky. They were not concerned with national security, only with attempting to preserve the cultural and ideological "purity" of the Marxist-Leninist system.

Looking back, I can see that my encounters with the KGB really had nothing to do with state security. Vladimir and Nikolay didn't think that either Brodsky or I was a spy or likely to do harm in any military or political sense to the system. Of course, Brodsky did do enormous harm to the system in a cultural and philosophical sense by his work. And I played a small part in that process through my translations of and commentaries on his work. What's *your* view of these things?

I don't have much experience with the KGB, I'm afraid.

Well, you're lucky. I can't say they ever beat me or tortured me, but of course they did change my life. They prevented my seeing Joseph for the next four years. And even after he emigrated, in June 1972, their "order" or "directive" prevented me from visiting the Soviet Union until 1991. They thus interrupted my contacts with A. F. Losev, who died in 1988, Tolya Naiman, and Zhenya Rein.

Chapter 4

The Poet in Exile: "I'll live out my days . . ."

Joseph Brodsky's American self-reinvention was radical and bold—and as the Cold War recedes more distantly into our past, a new generation has grown up that has no understanding of what he had to overcome. Let's begin with the beginning of his exile. When did you learn that Joseph was leaving the USSR?

The first I heard of Joseph's emigration was in late May. It was around his birthday, I guess, when Ellendea Proffer phoned to say that Carl was in Leningrad with him, and the news was that he was leaving Russia. As I recall, she told me the approximate date he was expected to reach Vienna.

She said that Carl would be back in Ann Arbor by the 25th, and I should phone him on the 27th. When I did, Carl and I agreed that he would fly to Vienna to meet Joseph and that I would be at our summer place on Goose Pond, near Tanglewood in the Berkshires. I'd be ready to spend at least a week with Joseph going over the translations I'd prepared for *Selected Poems*, most of which he hadn't yet seen.

It was, of course, heroic of Carl to fly to Vienna only nine days after having flown from Leningrad, via New York, to Detroit. But then, he was at least a dozen years younger, and correspondingly tougher, than I was.

Since I had spent several hours at Auden's home in Kirchstetten on June 21, 1970—following two or three earlier meetings in his New York apartment—I gave Auden's address and phone number to Carl and urged him to take Brodsky to meet Auden. Joseph had received Auden's "Foreword" in May 1970 from Michael Curran, to whom I had given it in a single-spaced, narrow-margin version that my wife had squeezed onto just two sheets of onionskin paper.

It's an odd foreword, hesitant, tentative, yet ending with this resounding affirmation: "After reading Professor Kline's translations, I have no hesitation in declaring that, in Russian, Joseph Brodsky must be a poet of the first order, a man of whom his country should be proud. I am most grateful to them both."[1]

Praise for Joseph, but praise for you, too. And who could have guessed in 1970 that two years later you would be waiting for Joseph at your summer cottage in the Berkshires, in western Massachusetts.

We sometimes didn't go at that time of year, because we shared it with my wife's sister and her family. So we arranged with them that we would have the place to ourselves. The Klines would be there early July and I would clear a week when I would have nothing else I had to do except pick up Joseph and then go over the translations with him.

Some of the writers who were doing Brodsky articles for the newsweeklies, like *Time* and *Newsweek*, perhaps others, called me. Well, I was already at Goose Pond.

I don't remember all the errors in the press but there were two that occurred often. One headline called him "Gulag Survivor."

It didn't stop in the 1970s. I found a 1990 Los Angeles Times *article, "The Poems of a Gulag Survivor," and a 1991* New York Times *article titled, "Joseph Brodsky Goes from Gulag to United States Poet Laureate."*[2] *But back then . . .*

People were saying, "Well, Brodsky who was in the Gulag . . ."

Rather than in internal exile, or psychiatric wards, which would have been accurate. The Gulag was a huge archipelago of prison camps.

---

1   Brodsky, *Selected Poems*, 12.
2   Jascha Kessler, "The Poems of a Gulag Survivor," *Los Angeles Times*, August 8, 1990; Irvin Molotsky, "Joseph Brodsky Goes from Gulag to U. S. Poet Laureate," *New York Times*, May 11, 1991.

One of them said he was in prison for, whatever, ten years. A lot of inaccuracies.

But how great the culture shock must have been when Joseph Brodsky landed in Detroit on July 9, 1972! Even in the late 1990s in Russia, there were still lots of shortages and the corner grocery store had only a few meager selections to sell under glass, and only one kind of soap.

That's right. He just couldn't take it. The grocery stores in London and Ann Arbor displayed not a can or two of soup, but twenty cans, not two or three bottles of *gazirovannaya voda* [soft drinks], but forty or fifty bottles.

Let's talk about that culture shock for a bit, and your observations when he arrived here straight from the USSR . . . well, via Vienna and London. He was starting from a staggering deficit, and the fact that he was able to get on his feet so quickly was . . . well, he did have help from people like you, but still, it was an astonishing achievement.

I agree. Absolutely. He was in deep culture shock for quite a while. I wonder about the difference between the pressure or the pain of scarcity and then the pressure—and in a sense also—the pain of abundance.

On a postcard written on the flight from Vienna to London, Joseph had scribbled: "My head is permanently turned to one side [as I look in shop windows]. Abundance is just as hard to take as poverty, maybe harder. The latter's preferable, because the soul is engaged. I personally can't take anything in— everything seems to bounce around, I've got spots before my eyes."[3]
That comment was written even before he arrived in America. He'd moved from a place with only one kind of laundry soap on the shelves to twenty.

That frustrated him. The relation between deficit and abundance in his world was suddenly reversed. In Russia, there had been a shortage of both goods and services but an overabundance of native Russian speakers— something much more essential than either goods or services for a *poet*. In

---

3   Lev Loseff, *Joseph Brodsky: A Literary Life* (New Haven: Yale University Press, 2011), 168.

the United States, there was an overabundance of both goods and services but a severe shortage of native Russian speakers.

Tell me about that plane he refused to board to Albany. He was planning to visit you in New York shortly after his arrival in Ann Arbor. At that point, you hadn't seen each other for several years.

Well, the flight he was booked for and didn't take was from Detroit to Albany. Detroit was the airport closest to Ann Arbor and Albany was the one closest to Goose Pond, where we had our summer cottage. He had been booked on the flight several days before he actually came. Carl told me that he very much wanted to see me and to see my translations—most of which he hadn't yet seen—but that he was in deep culture shock and felt he couldn't cope with yet another change of environment. He found everything overwhelming.

I don't even know whether he got to the airport on the day he had a reservation. I was expecting him to arrive at Albany. Then Carl Proffer called and said, "Well, he just can't handle it." Joseph very much wanted to see me and to see the translations, but simply couldn't face everything involved in the trip. The culture shock was deep, but he overcame it in a matter of weeks.

Shortly after he settled in Ann Arbor, Joseph finally did fly to Albany, the nearest airport to Goose Pond. You met him at the airport, and you hadn't seen each other for several years.

On July 21, Joseph boarded a plane in Detroit and landed in Albany at 10:54 a.m., where I met him and drove him to our cottage on Goose Pond. That's where and when I met him after four years of separation.

One of the first things I said was, "Well, this is the first time we've seen each other since . . . ," and then I said something like, "that time at the airport," meaning the airport in Leningrad. And I used the expression *v aeroporte*, the locative of airport. And he immediately corrected me, saying instead *v aeroportu*. I know I made lots of grammatical mistakes in Russian when I was talking to him at great length in Leningrad in '67 and '68, but he had never corrected me. I'm sure I had used a number of ungrammatical and unidiomatic expressions. I'm sure he sometimes smiled or maybe even chuckled at my grammar, but he'd never corrected me. But this time he did.

And then he sort of apologized and said, "I have to make sure I don't hear mistakes in Russian." Something like that. In other words, I used the wrong ending. I used "yeh" instead of "oo" and he didn't want to let that happen. So he was already feeling the isolation from the country where his language is the native language and he was afraid that he would lose it. I remember one of the most poignant lines in his poetry about himself, in the poem "1972," listed was what he was losing: "volosy, zuby, glagoly, suffiksy"—"I'll live out my days, losing gradually / hair, teeth, consonants, verbs, and suffixes. . . ." This change shows how deeply worried he was at the prospect of possibly losing "his verbs and suffixes."

The absolute control of his native language is essential to the poet. He was afraid of losing his total mastery of his native language.

Nevertheless, you made an island of peace for him in the Berkshires.

We spent six days together, from July 21 to July 26, much of it on the cottage deck or the treehouse deck, among tall pines and hemlocks, working together. At the end of it, he left Albany on a 10:40 a.m. flight on July 27. During the week we took a break from swimming, boating, and translation-checking to have a picnic at Tanglewood where we heard a wonderful concert by the Boston Symphony, conducted by Leonard Bernstein. Later Joseph became quite friendly with Bernstein.

But most of the time engaged in line-by-line scrutiny of my translations, most of which he hadn't previously seen.

What made the collaboration so harmonious?

I didn't have a poet's ego. I wasn't attempting to impose my own verse forms on Joseph's formal cadences, rhymes, and metrical patterns. And I was working from the original Russian, not a trot.

In this line-by-line scrutiny, did he find errors in your translations?

We found relatively few flat-out errors, but several cases where I had missed literary allusions or hidden quotations, and misread his intended tone. In more than one instance, I had failed to detect his gentle irony.

Can you give an example?

Here's one, from "To a Certain Poetess." I didn't detect the irony in the lines: "Kogda mne vyshli ot zakona 'vily,' / ia vashim proritsan'em byl sogret." I had translated them: "But when the Law put me in its disfavor / your bright predictions warmed my battered heart." When he pointed out my misreading, I reworked them to read: "And when the Law pitchforked me out of favor, / your dire prognosis cheered me up no end."

And flat-out errors?

Well, here's one. In "The Fountain," Joseph chuckled at my literal rendering of "l'vinyi zev" as "lion's jaw." Oddly, none of the Russians who had reviewed my translations had noticed this, and it seemed to work in context. However, Joseph pointed out that what he meant was "lion's maw"—a small flower, similar to a snapdragon.

In addition to running a fine comb over the translations you'd already done, did he bring any new poems for you to translate?

He had two poems written in February 1972, which he very much wanted to include in the *Selected*. He knew them both by heart, even the longer of them, which was seventy-two lines. He asked if I had a Cyrillic typewriter. He typed out the text of "Sreten'e'" [Nunc dimittis] on my manual portable, at a table on the deck. I hadn't seen either of the poems before. I began to translate this and the second poem "Odysseus to Telemachus" right away. These two powerful and moving poems are the final pages in the *Selected*.

Between the fall of 1972 and the following spring, when page proofs were returned and there wasn't a chance of any more revisions of my translations, we had plenty of opportunities to consult by letter, telephone, or in person. We appeared together at two or three dozen readings on various college campuses during this time. I also visited him in Ann Arbor for several days in mid-March. By late April, he had seen a set of page proofs and said he was delighted with the book. He added, "George, no one could have done a better job."

Pasternak said that perfect poetic translation was impossible, and competent translation enormously difficult. I know without Joseph's patient, informed, and sensitive collaboration, my own task would have been very tough indeed.

Which were your personal favorites in the fifty-or-so poems that make up the Selected?

At least twenty are particularly close to me, for various reasons: they are especially moving, they exhibit striking originality, historical insight, religious feeling, or human wisdom.

Here's the list: "Elegy for John Donne," "New Stanzas to Augusta," "On the Road to Scyros," "Refusing to catalogue all of one's woes," "Dido and Aeneas," "Postscriptum," "1 January 1965," "The Candlestick," "On Washerwoman Bridge," "September the First," "The Fountain," "Almost an Elegy," "On the Death of T. S. Eliot," "A Letter in a Bottle," "Einem alten Architekten in Rom," "Two Hours in an Empty Tank," "A Halt in the Desert," "Adieu, Mademoiselle Veronique," "Post Aetatem Nostram," "Nature Morte," "Nunc Dimittis," "Odysseus to Telemachus."

All of the poems in the *Selected* were written between 1960 and March 1972. Two others written in that period are "A second Christmas by the shore" in 1971 and "Letters to a Roman Friend" in 1972. I didn't get around to translating them until later; both are published in *A Part of Speech.*

I have the hardcover Harper & Row version of the Selected, *and also the Penguin* Selected, *published the same year. Why two?*

In March 1972, Frances Lindley, a vice president and senior editor at Harper & Row in New York, wrote me to suggest a hardcover United States edition of the British Penguin paperback. She'd already been in charge of the two Solzhenitsyn volumes Harper were to publish.

You're referring to the first volumes of the Gulag Archipelago *in the United States.*

I welcomed the move—and Joseph did, too. The edition was published in January 1974.

Harper & Row wrote that the notice on the volume had to be 1973, however, because that it was the first year in which it was published—albeit on the other side of the ocean.

Well, it was better than the Penguin edition, which had been published the previous November, in two ways: It had an index of titles and first lines, which Penguin had prepared but not used, since Nikos Stangos, the Penguin editor, argued that the other volumes in the series didn't have them.

And second, the type was photographically enlarged, which improved the appearance and readability. The pagination is unchanged.

It sold well, too—according to a letter Frances Lindley sent you on January 17, 1975, the book had sold just shy of 3,986 copies. Pretty good for a poetry volume's first year—especially considering that there was a Penguin edition that had just been published, too.

So it was a good year for Joseph's poems—two books in English. Not bad for the exile's first two years in America.

You're forgetting *Ostanovka v pustyne* [A halt in the desert] in 1970.

But that was a few years earlier.

The bigger point is, this and the *Selected* were the first books that Joseph had editorial control over. In the *Selected,* the poems, as well as their order and inclusion in one or another of the five parts, were chosen and decided by Joseph himself. It was a new experience for him.

His next volume of poetry in English, *A Part of Speech*, was published in 1980 by his new publisher, Farrar, Straus and Giroux. Several people did the translations—including Joseph himself. Ten of them were mine—and three were from the *Selected*: "Nature Morte," "Nunc Dimittis," and "Odysseus to Telemachus."

Did he ever criticize your translations during those early days of your collaboration in the United States?

The most common shortcoming that Joseph found in my translations during that week was that I missed his irony, and it was usually gentle irony. His irony was really never bitter or harsh the way much poetic irony is.

A Shadow over Goose Pond

Joseph Brodsky could be almost defiantly nonchalant about his change of address: "Perhaps exile is the poet's natural condition. . . . I felt a certain privilege in the coincidence of my existential condition with my profession."[4] *However, there was a darker side to Joseph Brodsky's arrival in America. In Loseff and Polukhina's*

---

4   Lev Loseff and Valentina Polukhina, eds. *Brodsky's Poetry and Aesthetics* (Basingstoke: Macmillan, 1990), 56.

A pensive Brodsky at a reading near Philadelphia, probably at Bryn Mawr or Haverford College, in October 1972. (Photo: Alan Hewitt)

book Brodsky's Poetics and Aesthetics, *your chapter includes a footnote on page eighty-seven:* "At this time Brodsky told me of his nightmare about repeating the fate of Marina Tsvetaeva who, after more than fifteen years of exile in Prague and Paris, returned to the Soviet Union in 1939 and took her own life in 1941."[5] *Wow. First of all, it's not entirely clear when this nightmare occurred.*

He told me that at Goose Pond, when he was there with us between July 21 and 27, 1972. I thought it was clear I was referring to that time.

It wasn't, but what did he say? That comment begs for some elaboration and detail.

He said precisely that. He said, "I have a nightmare about returning to Russia and ending the way Tsvetaeva did."[6] Of course, he said it in Russian, but he used almost exactly those words.

---

5   Ibid., 87n31.

6   Poet Marina Tsvetaeva (1892–1941) fled Soviet Russia in 1922, but returned to Moscow to join her husband Sergei Efron in 1939. Efron was arrested and later shot in prison on

Obviously, the nightmares were triggered because he, too, was in exile, as she had been, and might commit suicide? Or was he thinking more about her disastrous return to Russia after the safety of Prague and Paris?

You know, of course, that he loved Tsvetaeva and adored her poetry. Later he wrote wonderful things about it. In July 1972, he wasn't suggesting that he'd be going back to Russia in a month, or a year, or a few years. But early in his exile he stated: "I'm sure that some day I'll return to Russia." Of course he never did. Let's see, how long was Tsvetaeva in exile? She was in Germany, Czechoslovakia, and Paris from 1922 until 1939—seventeen years. He might have been thinking in terms of such a time frame, but he didn't give specific dates.

Perhaps he thought that he wouldn't be able to endure émigré life for more than ten or fifteen years, so he would go back to his beloved *rodina*—his homeland, the place of his birth. He had that yearning, which all Russians have, especially Russian poets when they go abroad, to return to their rodina. I think he really felt that he might eventually be pulled back. And, of course, he desperately missed his friends and especially his parents. Perhaps he was thinking that he might go back just so he could see his parents, because he knew they were getting old. As it turned out, both of them died before he received the Nobel Prize. And there was of course the pull of his native language. Does all that surprise you?

No, it doesn't surprise me . . . well, it does a bit.

You don't believe he really said those things?

It's just surprising because I think modern Americans, in general, underestimate how traumatic exile is. It's not something Americans readily identify with.

You mean the pull of the homeland?

No, I mean just being forced out of your country, and being unable to come back. The kinds of nightmares he was having, the trauma, and the culture shock.

October 16, 1941. Marina was evacuated with her son to Elabuga, Tatarstan, in 1941, where she lived in poverty and was harassed by the NKVD. She hanged herself on August 31, 1941.

I think Russians feel that pull to the homeland more than I suspect most Americans would.

So much of the world has been Americanized. I think it must mitigate the pull for us. It's relatively rare to be someplace where no one speaks any English. An American experiencing culture shock can always check into the Hilton— or simply go home. Other than a few pro-Soviet Americans during the Cold War . . .

Do you remember what Brodsky said in one of his essays about the Brit who became a Soviet spy?

Yes. Kim Philby.[7]

Joseph was in London and saw the front page of a British newspaper with the story about Philby. It displayed an enlargement of the postage stamp that the Soviets had issued in his honor "for his valued service to the Soviet Union."

It was the London Review of Books. *Joseph wrote about it at some length in his essay, "Collector's Item."*

Joseph really had a physical reaction, he was so disgusted, so horrified. He simply couldn't grasp that an Englishman had betrayed his country—a free country—in that way, and was receiving praise from those . . . he probably said "those goddamn Soviets."

Do you think I should have put that remark about his nightmares in the text, rather than putting it in a footnote?

Perhaps. It's a comment that requires a little amplification, just because it offers such a powerful window into his mind at that moment. But, you're the kind of guy who would put something disconcerting in a footnote—you have a gift for understatement.

---

7   Harold Adrian Russell Philby (1912–1988) was the most successful double agent of the Cold War period. While a high-ranking official within Britain's MI-5, he was working for the NKVD and later the KGB. He defected to the Soviet Union in 1963.

But keep in mind that my whole chapter in *Brodsky's Poetics and Aesthetics* was about the forms of Brodsky's exile, the variations on the theme of exile—hence, the footnote. But looking at both the text and footnote again, I see that you are right: I didn't make it clear that "this time" referred to the July 1972 week at Goose Pond.

Those days at Goose Pond sound magical and idyllic. And then it was over.

We said goodbye at the Albany airport on July 27. Ten weeks later, when I met his flight at the Philadelphia airport on October 4, I could see, over the five days we spent together giving readings at various campuses, that he had pretty much overcome any culture shock he had. He was already feeling very much at home in the United States.

The readings continued into 1975, and took Brodsky deeper into the America that would become his home.

Well I have a little story about one reading. I don't remember much else about it but it was on October 19th, 1973, and it was at the University of North Carolina in Chapel Hill. The senior Slavist there was a bald guy named Walter Vickery—nice fellow. It was pleasant weather. In North Carolina it was still mild. As I recall, it was a barbecue. In any case, we were eating outside, in other words eating *al fresco*. You can perhaps guess what's coming. Since Vickery, who was doing the cooking, was bald, I said quietly to Joseph, "Well, here we have *al fresco baldy*." Joseph liked that. Frescobaldi.

The seventeenth-century composer?

Yes.

A very tiny pun.

Yes, but he was amused by it.

He always liked puns. I once said that puns were the lowest form of wit. He looked at me, a little shocked and very earnest, and said, no, they showed a love of language.

About puns, I side with Joseph: I either gave him or told him about my 1974 essay "Philosophical Puns," and about my speculative suggestion—as a possible way of explaining the inexplicable power of rhyme in poetry—that certain rhymes function as "condensed philosophical puns." He was extremely enthusiastic about this idea: I recall his exact words: "Rifmy kak sokrashchennaia filosofiia. Genial'naia teoriia!" [Rhymes as abbreviated or condensed philosophy. A theory of genius!]

Was there anyone in particular that he wanted to meet, as he was discovering America? A whole new world had opened up for him.

One story from October 1972. Brodsky said, "There are two people I very much want to see, Berberova and Florovsky." Princeton was about an hour, an hour-and-a-half drive from my home in Ardmore, Pennsylvania. So I drove Joseph to Princeton to meet two distinguished Russian émigrés, Nina Berberova and Father Georges Florovsky. I had met Florovsky, of course, on several occasions. I don't remember what gift Joseph brought to him. He must have brought something. Anyway, Florovsky and his wife were very friendly and welcoming. We were there maybe an hour, maybe more. They served I'm sure Russian tea and cookies or something after Berberova served coffee.

Nina Berberova wrote a big book, which is out in English. I remember when it was first published in 1972. It's called *Kursiv moi* in Russian—*The Italics are Mine*. It's a good title. I haven't read it all, but I've found some fascinating things in it. She was married to Vladislav Khodasevich, and she knew Gorky, and so on.

I don't know if Berberova was still teaching at Princeton then. She had been teaching there. But I had been in touch with her, and later on she came and taught at Bryn Mawr and we co-taught. Not in the sense of being in the same room, but she taught one semester of Modern Russian Poetry and I taught the other. She taught Akhmatova and I taught Tsvetaeva, or vice-versa, that sort of thing. We got along very well, and we had a nice correspondence.

We stopped twice en route for Joseph to pick up wine and cognac, and he brought two or three bottles to hand to her. He'd already brought maybe one bottle of wine and then he said, "No, that's not enough. Let's stop at the next wine store and get something else." You probably know that Joseph liked to overwhelm people with generous gifts. The way he bought a fur coat, and God knows what else, for Vera Chalidze when she arrived in New York. Well, anyway, I remember few things about that day.

One felt that these were two—I don't want to say quite celebrities yet, but important people—were kind of testing out each other and sparring a little. Not unpleasantly at all. They were both pretty bright and they could make very good conversation.

I remember this: At some point, fairly early, maybe when we'd been there, I don't know, half an hour, Nina said—of course, all of it was in Russian: "Well, what if I serve some coffee?" or "Would you like some coffee?" And Joseph just lit up and said, "It would be staggeringly appropriate to have some coffee." I remember that hyperbolic expression. It's kind of a Brodskian phrase.

Afterwards, he said it was very interesting to meet her, and he wanted to see her again. But he added, "We were engaged in a kind of a ballet." That's the way he put it. "She was moving one way, and I was moving another way."

But about Nina, I guess the last book she wrote, or at least the last one that she gave me, was called *Zheleznaia zhenshchina*—"The Iron Woman." I don't know whether it ever got translated into English. Anyway, Joseph became very supportive of things that Nina was doing, including trying to get this book published in Russian or translated. I know he wrote letters to publishers.

And Florovsky?

As you may know, Florovsky had been born and raised in Russia and had left. He was in Paris during the 1930s teaching at that Russian theological institute, the Saint Sergius Institute of Orthodox Theology, where he was the professor of Russian philosophy and then later the dean at Saint Vladimir's Orthodox Theological Seminary in New York.

In 1937, I believe, he wrote a wonderful book, in some ways controversial called, in Russian, *Puti russkogo bogosloviia*, which is *The Ways of Russian Theology*. It's broader than that, really. It's about Russian religious thought.

Obviously, Brodsky had read at least some of it, and knew about this guy. Florovsky had also written about the church fathers, the Greek fathers, and so on. Brodsky must have known some of that, too. You never knew what people might have brought him or lent him or called to his attention. I told you that he had that volume of Nikolay Berdyaev on his desk when I was first in his room [in Leningrad]—*The Philosophy of the Free Spirit,* I think.

Did the meeting go well?

The priest's wife showed Brodsky the passage in the second volume of Nadezhda Mandelstam's Russian memoirs, which had just been published in Paris,[8] in which she praised Brodsky as "the best of the young poets who had gathered around Akhmatova." Do you have Max Hayward's translation? I liked Max and respected him a lot.

I do. She also wrote, "Among the crowd at Akhmatova's funeral there was one other mourner who also felt orphaned in a real sense: Joseph Brodski. Of all the younger friends who made life easier to bear in her last years, he was the most serious, honest, and selfless in his relations with her."

In the same paragraph—oh, she has a whole wonderful description of how he breathes and how his nostrils are involved. You remember she said, "He's not a human being. He's a wind orchestra."

The next paragraph but the same page: "I have heard Brodski read his verse. An active part in the process is played by his nose. I have never known anything like it before in all my life: his nostrils expand and contract and do all kinds of funny things, giving a nasal twang to each vowel and consonant. It is like a wind orchestra."

After that, she concluded with a sort of melancholy line. She says, "Well, whether he's a good poet or not, I don't know," or maybe she says, "It's too early to say, but that he's a poet, that's clear."

From the book: "Whether a good poet or not, the fact is that he is one, and this cannot be denied him. In our times it is hard luck to be a poet—and a Jew into the bargain."[9]

She didn't say "under this government," but that's really what she meant. "In this time, to be a poet and beyond that to be Jewish is not recommended." Then either before that or after that she says, "I fear that he will end badly." Do you remember that?

---

8   The Russian-language edition of the book *Vtoraia kniga* was published in 1972 by YMCA Press in Paris. It had circulated in samizdat before.

9   Nadezhda Mandelstam, *Hope against Hope* (Harmondsworth: Penguin, 1970), 123.

"He is, nevertheless, a remarkable young man who will come to a bad end, I fear."

Brodsky took that prediction calmly as well, saying "Eto normal'no." Florovsky's wife just handed it to him. I don't know if anybody read it aloud but in any case, Brodsky read it for the first time and they were looking to see how he'd react. And all he said was, "Eto normal'no." "That's normal."

He may have viewed his expulsion as a "bad end." And that "it is hard luck to be a poet—and a Jew into the bargain" may have stung. It was an odd thing to be a Jew in the USSR. How was he affected? His friend, Genrikh Steinberg, said: "Well my impression is not at all. It's like this, you hear a constant noise, and then you cease hearing it, it becomes a part of your subconscious, and emerges in your consciousness once it's over, when 'silence is the best thing I have ever heard.' . . . It's another thing when you are dealing with government agencies, the Party, the KGB, and the Ministry of the Interior. That is when you remember who is who, and if not, then you will quickly be reminded."[10]

Afterwards, Brodsky was so upset. I'd never seen him that upset. I forget how he put it, but he said, "That woman, she's not worthy of him. She's not good enough for him." He went on and on. He said he admired and respected Florovsky but he obviously didn't admire or respect Florovsky's wife.

I wonder if the whole visit stirred painful reminders that Nadezhda Mandelstam—who had become dear to him—was someone he would never see again. He last saw her on May 30, 1972, a few weeks before his emigration—and this incident at Princeton happened only a few months after. I remember, of course, his remarkable essay after her death in 1980, and its last paragraph: "Her wish came true, and she died in her bed. Not a small thing for a Russian of her generation. There are undoubtedly those who will cry that she misunderstood her epoch, that she lagged behind the train of history running into the future. Well, like nearly every other Russian of her generation, she learned only too well that the train running into the future stops at the concentration camp or at the gas chamber. She was lucky that she missed it, and we are lucky that she told us about its route."[11]

---

10 Polukhina, *Brodsky through the Eyes of His Contemporaries*, 2:132–33.

11 "Nadezhda Mandelstam (1899–1980)," in *Less Than One* (New York: Farrar, Straus & Giroux, 1986), 155–56.

But we can be glad that she was wrong in at least this one prediction.

She sure was. His future was brighter than anything Nadezhda Mandelstam could have foreseen. Brodsky became the leading poet of postwar Russia. His life and work continue to attract new readers and interest, here and abroad.

So let's talk about some of those early poems in exile. A year after his arrival, he lost a powerful protector, and the one who had written the influential foreword. And he wrote an elegy for the poet who had been a master of elegies, Wystan Auden. Not his first poem in English, but the first to be published and receive critical attention.

It's not quite so puzzling that Joseph would have written the "Elegy for W. H. Auden." He was intensely devoted to Auden and devastated by his death and wanted to say something poetic, so it's understandable. But in a way I guess it's not forgivable that he didn't realize how bad it was until two or three years later. We'll talk about that later.

And he began to collaborate actively, perhaps too assertively, with his translators.

However, it's *more* puzzling that he would do this about the translation of "1972." Note that this is one of the first translations identified as "by X with the author."

The "X" in this case being Alan Myers. That wasn't until seven years later in the Kenyon Review *in 1979.*

Interesting. I suspect the translation was turned down by the *New York Review of Books,* which had published Joseph's "Elegy for Auden," and perhaps by *Vogue,* which published my translation of "Nunc Dimittis" in 1973. The first book publication of "1972," as far as I know, was in 1980 in *A Part of Speech.*

Could it be, especially in the early days, that he wasn't writing for us?

What do you mean?

He wasn't writing for us, and hence wasn't so interested in what it sounded like in English. I mean "1972," notwithstanding its flaws in English, doesn't seem to be speaking to us, on this side of the ocean. Instead, he's saying "I'm not dead yet" to the Russians, by producing a major poem in exile. A major poem that, ironically, decries his decrepitude even as he flexes his poetic muscles.

Yes. I agree entirely. And note that this poem was dedicated to a *Russian*, his friend Viktor Golyshev, a gifted translator from English to Russian. Most of his other poems were dedicated to such non-Russians as Stephen Spender, Mark Strand, Derek Walcott, Margo Picken, Faith Wigzell, Véronique Schiltz, Brooke and Strobe Talbott, or Susan Sontag. Masha Vorobyov and Lev Loseff, to whom he dedicated other poems, were Russian émigrés. It's also relevant that my émigré poet friend, the poet Valentina Sinkevich, who knew the poems in *Ostanovka v pustyne* of 1970, considered "1972" Joseph's "most Russian poem."

That was the audience he still cared about. Especially in the early days he didn't know or care much about his audience here, because he had no idea what he was about to become.

You think so?

It's possible. I mean, the Nobel was in the future. The notion that he would be aspiring to be an English-language essayist would have seemed fantastic in the extreme. He had no idea he was about to be a powerful figure in the literary circles of New York City, nor that he was to become a global, cosmopolitan poet, American and broadly European as well. All this lay ahead in a future he couldn't possibly see.

How do you know that?

Because it's common sense. From Soviet Leningrad, he couldn't even have visualized New York City, and it would take years here to "get" its social, aesthetic, and political ecosystem. You've described his culture shock—it would take some time to reorient himself and conceptualize and grasp the possibilities in his new situation.

Well, you know another thing that would be interesting to date, and I really can't but I assume it was fairly early; was that little French rhyme that he probably quoted to more than one young woman, "Prix Nobel? Oui, ma belle." Of course it wasn't entirely serious. Brodsky said it, whether he made it up, I don't know. I doubt it. It could have been Tolia Naiman, because he knew French well and translated from French and Italian. As you know, they were very close, pretty much throughout Joseph's life, although there was some cooling toward the end.

I'm not entirely convinced that he didn't recognize the greatness in his own future.

You have a point on the Nobel, of course. Valentina Polukhina tells me that, in 1969, after his falling out with Nabokov over his poem "Gorbunov and Gorchakov," he pronounced that poem was the one that would earn him a Nobel Prize. That was when he was still in Leningrad.

She also says that he was first shortlisted for the Nobel as early as 1980, but he was pleased that his friend Czesław Miłosz won the prize instead. But here's a story from a year later, from his boss at Mount Holyoke, Prof. Joseph Ellis, replying to an email I sent him: "Joseph was a force of nature, the most intellectually interesting person I ever knew. As Dean of Faculty at Holyoke, I hired him into the Mellon Chair. When he asked me why I was willing to double his salary at Columbia, I said 'Because you're going to win the Nobel Prize.' He responded: 'How do you know that? I thought only I knew that.' It was 1981."

He finished with a charming detail: "Here's the inscription he wrote in my copy of Less Than One: *"To Joseph Ellis, from his humble namesake, or to the ringmaster from his animal. These notes toward a further blurring of old distinctions between art and life, good and evil, black and white, etc., etc., etc. April 18, 1986."*

But here's my point. He might have had an intuitive understanding of his future greatness, he wouldn't have been able to visualize the outlines and details of it, especially so soon after leaving Russia. It would have been more an article of faith than a plan.

You may be right. That's something that we could perhaps think about and discuss further.

Joseph Brodsky takes a break for a cigarette during a reading near Philadelphia in autumn 1972. (Photo: Alan Hewitt)

Back in those early days, everything about him was still kind of "Soviet." Hence the sensitivity in his poem "In the Lake District," about the place "where dentists thrive" and "their daughters order fancy clothes from London." After a lifetime of Soviet dental care and medical care—not to mention diet—when you go to a place, even as remote as Michigan, he must have felt kind of scruffy. He was, as he says, a man "whose mouth held ruins more abject / than any Parthenon." That was perhaps his first poem in exile, a month before "1972."

Did he seem scruffy to you?

No more than the rest of us in those days. But that's not the point. It's how it seemed to him. Presumably he saw himself as a reasonably dashing man relative to his circle of Petersburg peers, then suddenly he was transported to a place where his teeth were substandard and his health was crummy. It probably did make him feel old. In "1972"—when he's only thirty-two, mind you!—he writes:

> *Aging! Hail to thee, senility.*
> *Blood flows as slowly as chilly tea.*

And then continues:

> *As for my dental cave, its cavities*
> *rival old Troy on a rainy day.*
> *Joints cracking loud and breath like a sewer,*
> *I foul the mirror. It's premature*
> *to talk of the shroud. But you may be sure,*
> *those who'll carry you out besiege the doorway.*

Well that's a good point. I hadn't really thought of it that way. You were his student, did he seem old to you? How old was he when you were taking his classes?

That was a few years later. He'd had time to get his teeth pulled.

Right, but you said he was still under forty.

Yes.

And he asked you to call him "Joseph." He never did that until he was forty or something.

Ludmila Shtern said that, and she was wrong. He was thirty-six, thirty-seven when I met him. I guess I can claim to be one of the girls "In the Lake District."

By the way, have you actually looked over the translation of "1972"?

It's a magnificent poem, and certainly a lot gets lost in English. There are some lines that ring through even in translation:

> Aging is growth of a new but a very fine
> hearing that only to silence hearkens.

But compared to the Russian?

It's pretty bad and I don't know whom to blame. But I've studied it closely. The Russian text is splendid, but it's probably the most challenging to translate of any of Joseph's poems, certainly till that date. This is because of such original and powerful features as "destructive" triple dactylic rhymes and slant rhymes. I'm not sure that anyone could have produced an adequate English version. Certainly "Alan Myers with the author" didn't manage to. One of the most powerful phrases in this powerful poem is the list of the things he is losing: "volosy, zuby, glagoly, suffiksy." I've already discussed how he corrected me at the airport, which shows how deeply worried he was at the prospect of possibly losing "his verbs and suffixes."

He described Ann Arbor as "a small town proud to have made the atlas," though I believe its population was about 100,000 at the time—probably small compared to Leningrad, which was over four million. Yet he conquered New

York, too—which was double that, and endlessly complex with its boundless energy, aggressive creativity, cutthroat circles of influence and power, its ethnic neighborhoods, restaurants, and slums.

He certainly did.

Even many Americans couldn't function effectively in New York, with its hepped-up energy, restless intelligence, and endless drive. As a former Soviet citizen, a school dropout at fifteen, it was quite a feat to become a recognized poet and power broker in the New York literary world in a few short years.

There were some fights along the way, as you know.

Oh lots. The fact that he navigated a sort of carnivorous literary world . . .

That was astonishing. I agree. I saw it at various stages. Well, in one sense, he was very lucky in that there were two or three émigré Russians who read his poetry before most of it was translated. They recognized his quality and could do something about it.

For Joseph, the most important of the Russian émigrés was Alex Lieberman. He had enormous cultural power. He became very important in the whole Condé Nast empire of publications like *Vogue* and *Mademoiselle*, which is why an important early Brodsky translation appeared in their pages.

I wondered about that history when I was working on Joseph Brodsky: Conversations. *One of the first mass media interviews that dealt with him as a poet rather than as a exiled dissident was "A Poet's Map of His Poem: An Interview by George L. Kline," which included your translation of "Nunc Dimittis," as well as your interview with him about it. It was published in* Vogue *in September 1973.*

He gets a lot of credit for his success, but he was also incredibly lucky. There might not have been a Lieberman or composer Vladimir Ussachevsky. And not only Ussachevsky, but his wife Betty Kray, who was the executive secretary of the Academy of American Poets in New York, which invited Joseph and me to read there in late October 1972.

You and Joseph were indeed lucky. Kray was a legendary visionary advocate of poetry. Stanley Kunitz called her "the moving spirit behind most of the programs and activities that have made New York the poetry capital of the United States and an international poetry center." And lucky with Lieberman. Publishing in Vogue *or* Mademoiselle *was a revolutionary choice—for both of you, for anyone, really.*

I never thought of submitting anything to either of those magazines—but I got a request from Lieberman or someone speaking for Lieberman. I never published there before—and I never published there afterwards. Why would I? It was a unique and important coincidence, or maybe just lucky. I don't know how many people read those magazines, but it's a lot. They're wide circulation, read by people who care about fashion, who tend to be interested in the arts. Not a bad place to publish—it just never occurred to me.

Did you observe anything in Brodsky that prefigured his determination not only to survive, but to thrive so spectacularly?

I don't know. Have you read the book, I suppose you have, by David Bethea? I think he speaks to this question in *Joseph Brodsky and the Creation of Exile*.

I marked a wonderful passage here. He quotes Brodsky: "To be an exiled writer is like being a dog or a man hurtled into space in a capsule (more like a dog, of course, than a man, because they will never bother to retrieve you). And your capsule is your language. To finish the metaphor off, it must be added that before long the passenger discovers that the capsule gravitates not earthward but outward in space."

Then Bethea adds: "The utopian writes in hopes that the capsule will gravitate earthward; the poet follows his own lonely, centrifugal trajectory. In the final analysis Brodsky is, like Tsvetaeva, an exile among exiles. He stands alone, neither a character in the primal scene of someone else's family romance nor a rebel in the square of someone else's political unconscious. He chooses his own roles and takes responsibility for the success or failure of the performance."

He calls this Brodsky's "creation of exile," which he italicizes. The book was published in 1994, and he writes "with the coming of the post-glasnost era and the inevitable demise of the 'bardic mode' in Russian literature. Joseph

Brodsky may be the last great poet in the tradition about whom it can be said that he created himself and in turn was created *by what he wrote." Quite a statement. No wonder he had those nightmares.*[12]

Yes, the passage from Bethea's "Polemical Introduction" is the one I had in mind. What Bethea has to say there strikes me as both perceptive and profound. And it emphasizes what I've been arguing, namely, that Brodsky as a great Russian poet and a great English essayist was self-created, despite minor help along the way from such as Ussachevsky, Lieberman, Yury Ivask, and me.

Well, I don't want to try to psychoanalyze Joseph but obviously he had some kind of an inner spark or flame.

A spark that needed guidance and direction. That's why I find your July 2, 1972, letter to Elizabeth Kray, executive director of the Academy of American Poets, as you mentioned earlier, so interesting—a letter written on the very day he was flying from London to Detroit. I guess they were trying to market him at some point like Voznesensky?

From your letter:

> *I'm delighted to accept your generous offer to extend the Brodsky readings to a second evening and am sure that Iosif will be too. . . . The honoraria which you mention are quite acceptable to me and will be, I feel certain, to Iosif.*
>
> *Mr. Auden, I'm sure, meant well when he wrote to Mrs. Selma Warner about booking Iosif for readings. And perhaps at that time Iosif was feeling financial pressures. But now he has had several publishers' advances (e.g., for a German edition from Piper Verlag) and will shortly be receiving a good salary from the University of Michigan, so he isn't really in need of money. Furthermore, Auden was probably thinking in the familiar (to him) terms of whirlwind Voznesensky-type junkets, for which the services of Mrs. Warner may indeed be necessary. But Iosif's case is drastically different: he is a private and "hermetic" poet, a "poet's poet," not a public or theatrical poet. Mrs. Warner would tend to set his fees at Voznesensky level ($1,000 to $1,500 per reading), which would effectively price Iosif out of the academic market, on which he must rely for the long term. I am confident that for these and other reasons Iosif will not want to be "managed" by Mrs. Warner or her agency.*

---

12   David M. Bethea, *Joseph Brodsky and the Creation of Exile* (Princeton: Princeton University Press, 1994), 46, 47.

But of course he will have to make that decision himself when he reaches this country, between July 5 and 10. Meantime, I beg you to keep the Academy readings at the Donnell Library Center.

Yes, well don't you think I was right to protest about a possible Warner involvement?

Oh yes, with the obvious proviso that 1,000 dollars is a trifling sum in today's dollars. Certainly it was the right move. Your concerns are especially warranted given the next passage in this letter: "You may not be aware that Voznesensky was scheduled at the University of Michigan and at another (distant) campus on the same evening last fall." The no-show "left the people at the U. of Michigan frustrated and angry enough to contemplate bringing suit against Mrs. Warner and her agency. I feel that it is imperative to avoid such contretemps in Iosif's case."

That, too. It seemed clear to me that Joseph wouldn't want to be managed by Mrs. Warner, who would charge universities or places like the YMHA in New York $1,000 or $1,500 for a reading.

But that puts you in quite a crucial position, in an early moment of his career. Had you not written that, had you not been there to intervene, I think his career would have taken a very different path.

Tell me more about what you mean.

We take it for granted now, but this early stage it was more precarious than it looks in retrospect. It might not have taken shape the way it did had he started touring the country and speaking in large auditoriums for $1,500 a pop, Yevtushenko style.

That's a very good point. I confess that I hadn't thought of it that way.

If he had been marketed like Yevtushenko or Voznesensky, everything might have been very different.

I suppose that could have happened, especially since he revered Auden and he would have taken Auden's advice very, very seriously. In a sense, I had to talk him out of following Auden's advice.

His unconventional success as an academic is startling for somebody who dropped out of school at fifteen.

And he was very worried that, having no advanced degrees, he wouldn't be able to teach a university course. I reminded him of how in Leningrad in 1967 he had given me a fascinating lecture on the history of poetry in his native city in the 1950s and after. I could tell from that experience that he was a gifted, natural teacher, and I think I persuaded him of that fact.

Yevtushenko, too, eventually made a career as an American academic. Joseph would pave the way—ironically enough, given his reservations about him. In those early years, however, academia might have taken a step back from Brodsky. In his initial bewilderment after arriving in the United States, he certainly would not have had a grasp of the cultural context and implications of his choices in this regard.

You're modest. I admire that. But without your intervention, it might have gone a different way—and perhaps not just for him.

I want to give him all possible credit for the success he had. He certainly deserved it. But I helped a little bit along the way. I'll admit that.

Much later, you helped him in another significant way. You also had a role in promoting his work with the Swedish Academy, didn't you?

It was before 1987, but perhaps only a year or two years before, that I received a letter from the Swedish Academy.

They wanted me to send them some poems. I don't recall whether they identified specific poems or just some poems they had heard about that I had translated, that hadn't yet been published. I sent them the Russian texts and my translations of two or three poems. At that point, the only translations I had finished but not yet published were "Eclogue V" and "An Admonition." But I had also completed a few of the sonnets to Mary Queen of Scots and may have sent them, though they were never published. In any case, it was clear that Joseph was on the short list for the Nobel Prize. How short it was, I don't know.

Finding the letters is probably not going to be too easy. My wife keeps saying that she opens up a box somewhere and it's nothing but unfiled, unorganized correspondence. But I'd like to remind you of a way I helped

Joseph after the letter to Betty Kray but long before the exchange with the Swedish Academy. It was during that week at Goose Pond in late July.

The Loneliness of His Work, the Brightness of His Life

How was Joseph different in those early days, compared to his later life? How different was he then from what he became? When you were talking about those languorous days at Goose Pond, I remembered something from Irena Grudzińska Gross's book: "In 1994, when he was forced to visit a cardiologist during his stay in Sweden, he told him that he felt like a wounded animal who simply tried to survive. He expected to die any time; when he was leaving his hotel room, he would put his papers in order. 'Hurry sickness' was the diagnosis of the psychologist who interviewed him on that occasion."[13]

What's "hurry sickness"?

Extreme time-urgency and always rushed and putting tons of pressure on himself. Irena told me that she had actually seen this remarkable document, so it's not hearsay.

That's who he eventually became—one of those very driven people who always have a sense that they are running out of time. Indeed they are. Indeed all of us are. But was he like that in those early days? What was he like?

Yes, I'd say he was definitely more relaxed. You've seen the lovely photographs of the two of us, published with my little essay "Translating Brodsky" in *Bryn Mawr Now* in 1974. You can see that Joseph and I are very relaxed and enjoying each other's company, actually laughing in one of the photos.[14]

I would say on the one hand, of course, as an exile he missed his friends and he especially missed his parents. I think he was, despite his initial culture shock, feeling free and able to write what he wanted to, expecting that it would be published. There has been a lot written about his early years in exile, some of it I think nonsense.

---

13   Irena Grudzinska Gross, *Czeslaw Milosz and Joseph Brodsky: A Fellowship of Poets* (New Haven: Yale University Press, 2009), 113.
14   The photo Kline mentions is on the cover of this volume.

George Kline introduces Joseph Brodsky before a reading in the early 1970s.

What parts do you think were nonsense?

Wasn't it Keith Gessen in the *New Yorker,* reviewing the Loseff literary biography, who said something like, "In America, Brodsky was terribly alone." Do you remember something like that?

Over the years, I remember a lot of media portrayals of Byronic stances, the sighing poet gazing out at the lonely sea. The Gessen passage you're referring to is probably this one:

> *Brodsky's poems during his first years in the States are filled with the most naked loneliness. "An autumn evening in a humble little town / proud of its appearance on the map," one begins, and concludes with an image of a person whose reflection in the mirror disappears, bit by bit, like that of a street lamp in a drying puddle. The enterprising Proffer had persuaded the University of Michigan to make Brodsky a poet in residence; Brodsky wrote a poem about a college teacher. "In the country of dentists," it begins, "whose daughters order clothes / from London catalogues, . . . / I, whose mouth houses ruins / more total than the Parthenon's, / a spy, an interloper, / the fifth column of a rotten civilization," teach literature. The narrator comes home at night, falls into bed*

with his clothes still on, and cries himself to sleep. That year, Brodsky wrote a
poem indicating that, in being forced to leave Russia, he lost a son.[15]

We're back to the bad teeth, again.

The *Collected* lists "Odysseus to Telemachus" as written in March 1972, two months before his departure, perhaps anticipating it—he had already received an "official" invitation to emigrate from the fictitious Ivri Yakov in Israel. But the estrangement with his son had already begun in the USSR, really, there had already been a number of separations.

Well, Gessen left out a lot. And he fails to distinguish, as Joseph Ellis of Mount Holyoke clearly did in his moving obituary notice, between the darkness, including loneliness, of Joseph's *work* and the brightness and warmth of his *life*. I would take exception only to Ellis calling Joseph an "atheist." But of course it was a rhetorical flourish, in contrast with Joseph identifying *The Book of Common Prayer* as "the beginning."

It took some time for Joseph Ellis to dig out this reference, but he finally found
it for me. After noting that Joseph tended to interject "well" when he was
"groping for the least offensive English word," he told this anecdote:

> *Though the mundane business of recording grades never captured his fullest*
> *attention, he regarded the classroom (and not the chapel) as the only sacred*
> *spot on the premises. "They cannot write. Well, because you see, well, they*
> *have read nothing. You know, well, it is, whatever." These words delivered*
> *by the erstwhile Mellon Professor of Literature after a particularly bad class*
> *while stomping around my office in a hat that looked like a relic from what*
> *he called his Siberian phase. I said, "That's why you're here, Joseph. To teach*
> *them." A long pause. Several quick drags on his cigarette while he gazes out*
> *the window. Then the cat smile all over his face, the Russian bear hug, the bolt*
> *towards the door. "Of course, of course, well, yes, well. We must start at, well,*
> *the beginning." I trailed him down the hallway and yelled, "By the way, what*
> *is the beginning?" He giggled, "Of course the* Book of Common Prayer." *This*
> *from a Jewish atheist.*[16]

---

15   Keith Gessen, "The Gift," *New Yorker,* May 23, 2011.
16   Joseph Ellis, *Mount Holyoke College Alumnae Quarterly* (Spring 1996). The tale has
      a curious coda. On May 27, 2018, in a widely shared series of tweets on Twitter, the
      poet and former Amherst student Matthew Zapruder wrote: "I also had Brodsky in

People saw different aspects of him. Have you read Ludmila Shtern's *A Personal Memoir*?

Yes, I reviewed it, also in the Kenyon Review.

In some ways it's very nice, very interesting, although it had all kinds of mistakes in it. I guess I told you I read the proofs so I was able to correct some errors and supply some omissions. It's very good and fills in a lot of things that nobody has filled in about his relations in Leningrad with various people and his relations with Russian émigrés in this country. It says nothing about all the Americans—including major American and British poets—who became his friends.

Well for one thing the people, the Americans, he had met in Leningrad. Carl and Ellendea Proffer, Strobe and Brooke Talbott, Sam Ramer, Dick Sylvester, Peter Viereck, Mike Curran, Jim Billington, the list goes on. I could probably name a dozen.

He sought them out and in many cases became very friendly, extremely friendly with Peter, as you know, with me, and with some others. He was very good at—how shall I put it?—judging people and feeling almost at first contact that they were good people, serious people, intelligent, knowledgeable, perceptive, and he wanted to be with them, to be their friends. There weren't very many people like that.

He did that again on almost first contact with Seamus Heaney, Derek Walcott, Mark Strand, Dick Wilbur, Susan Sontag, and Bob Silvers. Probably a couple of others that I've forgotten.

I noticed that. In Shtern's book, the clock pretty much stops when he comes to America, but the same is true in Loseff's book.

What do you mean?

---

college and he got up, lit a cigarette, stood by the window looking out at the snow and said, 'I am tempted to dismiss class right now.' He was wearing a green velour suit. This is still one of the top ten moments in my life. . . . And then he told us all if we didn't figure out the answer to my question by the next class that he would cancel the rest of the semester. That is the god's honest truth." Zapruder's question? "What the Book of Common Prayer was. He was saying poetic cultures each have certain texts with a huge influence: they are absorbed by the most important poets, such as Dickinson, for whom BCP was central: we can trace its rhythms through her work then [sic] contemporary American poetry." Zapruder concluded: "even at the time I recognized it was a great moment and I really learned something for once." Another

Well, Loseff gives us a detailed and nuanced examination of the Russian trial and internal exile, but then the American part of his life is only a third of his book. He deals with his marriage in passing, in a single sentence. The American years rush by as if they were just some sort of coda, yet it was a period that was in its own way deep and rich with important friendships, and it formed the bulk of his poetic career.

He said once—you've probably heard this, he probably said it more than once; he said it in my presence in Stockholm to a German publisher—"Well, I choose my friends very carefully." The implication was that there were only a handful of friends, which in a sense is true—maybe a dozen. That was a prelude to his saying, "and one of the best and most important of them is Tomas Venclova." I was going to come back to this later, but he went on to deliver a very strong pitch to the German publisher saying, "You definitely should bring out a book of German translations of Venclova's poetry."

Joseph was certainly an important supporter of Tomas Venclova at a critical time. I'm thinking in particular of the occasion on May 11, 1975, when the Lithuanian poet applied to the Central Committee of the Lithuanian Communist Party for permission to leave the country. Nearly a year later, on April 1, 1976, Brodsky wrote in the New York Review of Books, *"Since then nothing has been heard about him, and in the light of events described in available documents one fears for his future." He continued:*

> Tomas Venclova is a Lithuanian, which makes things worse, because very few Americans have any idea where Lithuania is. Sparing you a geography and history lesson, let me state that Mr. Venclova is the best poet living on the territory of that empire of which Lithuania is a small province. I dare to state

---

former student, the journalist and film critic Oliver Jones, tweeted: "In my class, Brodsky made you memorize a poem and write it during class as a quiz. I got every word correct, but I wrote in all caps and didn't put the punctuation in. He gave me an F. It was glorious." Zapruder also recalled other examples less worthy of admiration: "We all started smoking in class too. It was awesome. He stole my friend Amy's lighter once. The best part was, he smoked Vantages, which are the ones with the special hole in the filter, which makes you wonder why he bothered if he was going to rip them out." According to Viktor Golyshev, "When I was in America, Brodsky showed me the list of books that were required reading for his students. There were some 300 titles, beginning with *Gilgamesh* and ending with Joyce. I was shocked: 'It's impossible to read this!' He merely shrugged: 'It doesn't matter, let them try.'" Polukhina, *Brodsky through the Eyes of His Contemporaries*, 2:195.

this evaluation of his work because I am acquainted with it perhaps more than anyone else in this hemisphere, since I have translated his poetry into Russian.[17]

This excerpt does not convey the sharpness and poignancy of Brodsky's short piece in the urgent situation. He concluded: "We need to act efficiently and at much earlier stages. Any defense takes much longer than the prosecution, and time is not a good thing any more when it is at the disposal of the state."

Joseph was trying very hard to help Tomas and, to some extent, I'm sure he did. Nasty things were appearing about him in the press. The guy could have been tossed into the slammer, or sent into exile somewhere for what he'd written and what he'd said, and whom he was seeing, and so on.

How did you meet him? Presumably after his emigration in 1977.

Joseph brought us together. I first heard about him when I was with Brodsky in Leningrad. Before he was in this country, Joseph urged me to translate one of his poems. It's the one dedicated to Mandelstam, called "In Memory of a Poet."[18] Joseph said this guy is a major poet of our times, a major twentieth-century poet, and I think that's probably true. Of course, I responded to some of the themes in the poem I translated. I don't know a word of Lithuanian but I was working with a couple of Lithuanian émigrés to translate.

I'm sure I would have recalled meeting him in any of my visits to Russia, including the two times that I saw Joseph in Leningrad in '67 and '68.

How did Tomas strike you when you first met him. What were your impressions?

Well, he's quiet and calm and not fiery—dignified, certainly. He has gravitas.

Tomas and I generally spoke English together, but certainly in our first two or three or four meetings, we spoke only in Russian. There was a time, probably in the late seventies, when Tomas wanted to speak English, and he quizzed me on the adequacy of his English. His English is fine now, as it wasn't earlier.

---

17   Joseph Brodsky, "Fate of a Poet," *New York Review of Books,* April 1, 1976.
18   Kline's draft translation of this poem is included in Chapter 10.

What drew you to Tomas Venclova's poetry? What did you see about it from the beginning?

I'd read it in Joseph's translations, which were wonderful. Joseph had told me a lot about it.

He sent me two of his books, let's see, what are the titles of his books? There's a book of poetry then there's a book of prose.

Winter Dialogue.

Yes, right, that's one of them. They're very interesting, very lively, very well written and very perceptive.

I've said to him more than once I would love to sit in on a course of his. In Berlin, he was teaching Pasternak and Tsvetaeva all the poets that Joseph and I love. And he's written about all of these poets in his dissertation, which has never been translated. I've read some of it. It's a lovely work.

He also wrote me very nice things about Zak Ishov, as he'd gotten to know Zak, had him in class, in seminar, but also know him as a person. "Zak and I are developing a very warm relationship, and I respect him a lot. I'm very fond of him." Things like that.

What else did Joseph say about Tomas?

I can tell you one thing, I've been thinking about this and thinking about how you would translate it and I'm not quite sure. The word is *solnyshko*. It's from the word *solntse*, which means "sun." It's a word of endearment that you can use for either a man or woman. I've heard Joseph say it to only two people. In my presence, he said it only to Tomas.

Some of the tsar's family used this word *solnyshko* in their correspondence. Sometimes it's translated "sunny," but that doesn't really make any sense in English. I don't know how to translate it, really. It's more like a person who is very dear, very precious.

In Russian, as in other languages and cultures, the sun can be a kind of metaphor for a major cultural figure or movement. When Pushkin died, there were headlines that said the sun of Russian poetry had set or died out. I think there were some headlines when Joseph died that used, *solntse*, the sun.

We spoke a moment ago about the clock stopping for many Russians when Joseph arrived in America. That reminds us of an important clock that didn't stop. You attended the Nobel award ceremonies in Stockholm in December 1987. You must have been euphoric.

I was in my car when I heard the news on the radio. I just about went through the roof. I reached him in London to say "Congratulations, Joseph!" to which he responded, "And congratulations to you, too, George!"

He was acknowledging your role in getting the Nobel. A memorable conversation indeed!

It's certainly one of the most memorable. Two others: In 1977, I had called him in Ann Arbor to congratulate him on his newly acquired United States citizenship. More than a decade later, I phoned him on his birthday in Athens. He had just returned from Istanbul and vividly described what he had witnessed there: "Warships of the Third Rome steaming past the Second Rome on their way to the First Rome." Later he included this observation in his essay, "Flight from Byzantium." That is, Moscow, the Third Rome and the former Constantinople as the second.

It was a timely award. Glasnost and perestroika were making their appearance in his homeland.

All the more so because he had been in such poor health, I was afraid the Nobel Committee might realize too late that he deserved the prize. So yes, I was invited to Stockholm and very grateful. I was on top of the world.

Chapter 5

The "Good Lexicon" Rule

In our earlier conversations, you've described your friendship with Joseph Brodsky and your long collaboration together. In a 1974 piece in The Slavic Review, *Helen Muchnic wrote this about it: "George Kline, collaborating with the poet, has translated most of his published work. He has done this with exemplary modesty and sensitiveness, and as successfully as anyone I know. The introduction he has supplied is an admirable piece of criticism, and his 'Note on the Translation' is a model of good sense."*[1]

"On the Death of Zhukov" was singled out for particular praise. John Bayley, writing in the *Los Angeles Times,* spoke of how I had "miraculously managed to preserve" the meter and beat, with a pause or rest in the middle of each line.[2]

Joseph had certainly expressed pleasure with your translations. In his dissertation, your friend Zak Ishov cites a note to you—half in Russian, half in English, scrawled in the margins of a manuscript with six new translations:

> *Dear George, I am greatly delighted: it came out wonderfully. To hell with the rhymes, if it works out this way. The only thing that makes me sad is the impossibility of paying you back, for I can't do anything adequate for you. Forever yours, Joseph. I think that I am terribly lucky. Excuse me, please, my*

---

1   Helen Muchnic, review of *Selected Poems* by Joseph Brodsky, trans. George L. Kline, with foreword by W. H. Auden, *Slavic Review* 33, no. 4 (1974): 837–38.

2   John Bayley, "The Brodsky Paradox," *The Los Angeles Times*, October 29, 2000.

terrible English. But I should like to say you the following: remember I respect and love you. . . . From my point of view you are a big man.[3]

Let's explore some of your approaches to translation, beginning with a summary of your experience collaborating with Joseph in these pre-Nobel days. Many others have shared their memories of working with him, but you're the earliest of his English translators, the man who brought Joseph Brodsky into English.

It was a unique experience. I was working closely with a Russian poet who had a deep, subtle, and also fallible, command of my language—the language I was struggling, with his help, to bring his poems into. It was always stimulating, sometimes illuminating, but occasionally frustrating and humbling. I learned which alternatives will *not* work, and why. And this can be as heady an experience as the one of attaining, with Joseph's help, clear improvements in one's imperfect English versions of his more recalcitrant Russian texts.

The collaboration in those early days was very harmonious. Ellendea Proffer Teasley, in Brodsky Among Us, *wrote "Translation was something mystical for Joseph." He had learned of many literatures through translation, and, as we have discussed, was himself a translator. How did that collaboration work?*

He would raise a question. He would say this line isn't right or that's not the right word or you've missed the irony. Something would be wrong with the line and I'd say, "Okay, I understand what you mean," and I would rewrite the line, and then he'd approve it. I can give you specific examples of several of these. In some cases we went through two or three alternative lines before agreeing on one of them. In at least one case we circled through a few lines only to agree in the end that the line we had started with was the right one. From 1972 until at least 1979, that process worked beautifully. Joseph was never impatient or domineering—until the 1980s. There were even a few cases where he made acceptable suggestions himself. When we were

---

3   Cited in Zakhar Ishov, 'Post-horse of Civilisation': Joseph Brodsky Translating Joseph Brodsky. Towards a New Theory of Russian-English Poetry (PhD diss., Free University of Berlin, 2008), 81. Letter dated Easter 1969 from Brodsky Papers, Beinecke Rare Books and Manuscripts and Library, Box 19 Fld. 50. The letter was written on Easter 1968 in the margins of the manuscript of the English publication: "Joseph Brodsky, Six New Poems," trans. George L. Kline.

Joseph Brodsky teaching at the University of Michigan, spring 1973. (Photo: Terrence McCarthy)

Joseph Brodsky struggles to explain a thought to his Ann Arbor students, spring 1973. (Photo: Terrence McCarthy)

working on "A second Christmas . . . ," he was the one who suggested a slant rhyme that I was happy to accept, namely "unfrozen/horizon."

On the other hand, his 1974 poem "On the Death of Zhukov" has a complex ending, containing an embedded reference to Derzhavin's 1800 poem "Snegir'" [The bullfinch] on the death of Suvorov. The last four lines are especially difficult to put into English. Joseph wrote out and sent me a totally different version from what I'd sent or shown him. I found it quite unacceptable, and told him so. In those days he didn't insist on his version. He didn't say, "George, you've got to use my lines," for this reason or that.

You had several other specific examples in the piece you wrote, "Revising Brodsky," in a book Translating Poetry: The Double Labyrinth, *edited by your friend Daniel Weissbort. Perhaps you could share one of these instances.*

Two stanzas in "Nature Morte" gave us headaches. I'll talk about one of them. The poem first appeared in the *Saturday Review* on August 9, 1972 before it appeared in the *Selected.* The rhyme scheme of the original is ABAB, however, we translated throughout XAYA, where X and Y are non-rhyming masculine endings.

In the first stanza of the third section:

Joseph Brodsky discusses poetry with his students at the University of Michigan, Spring 1973. (Photo: Terrence McCarthy)

Кровь моя холодна.
Холод ее лютей
реки, промерзшей до дна.
Я не люблю людей.

My blood is very cold—
its cold is more withering
than iced-to-the-bottom streams.
People are not my thing.

He didn't like the unsteady masculine line with the rhyme, "withering/ thing," but his main objection was the 1960s American slanginess of "people are not my thing"—although "thing" can perhaps be justified in this particular poem. The literal is the unslangy "Ia ne liubliú liudéi"—that is, "I don't like people."

So I began changing the second line and moving "than" to line two. Then I suggested several alternative fourth lines, ending with a slant rhyme for "than." They included "I dislike everyone," "People I cannot stand," and "People don't turn me on." The last one has the same whiff of the 1960s. I tended to favor the second, despite its slightly awkward inversion. It looked like this:

My blood is very cold—
its cold is fiercer than
iced-to-the-bottom streams.
People I cannot stand.

When that didn't pass muster with Joseph, I offered a hybrid second revision:

My blood is very cold—
its cold is more withering
than iced-to-the-bottom streams.
I dislike everyone.

The slant rhyme "wither*ing*/every*one*" is dubious. In the end we returned reluctantly, as a *pis aller,* to the original version.

The Poem Brodsky Regretted

To celebrate National Poetry Month in 2013, The New York Review of Books *has posted poems and articles by writers who have appeared in its pages over the years. Joseph Brodsky was among those chosen. The first poem published in its series was his "Elegy to W .H. Auden," one of his early poems written in English, rather than Russian. Not his best by a long shot.*

I hadn't seen that issue of the *New York Review*. What you tell me about it stirs up mixed feelings. On the one hand, I'm glad that the editors are paying attention to Brodsky at a time when some people appear to have forgotten him. On the other hand, I deeply regret that they chose to reprint his 1973 "Elegy for Auden," the first serious poem he wrote in English, one that in a few years he loudly and publicly renounced. It simply doesn't work as an English poem. Bad.

I'm surprised that Ann Kjellberg, his friend and defender, and the executor of the Brodsky estate, approved it. She knows better. Let's hope the editors will reprint something better next, either Joseph's 1977 "Elegy: For Robert Lowell" or a decently translated poem from the dozen years after 1973. A small point in the *Review* introduction: *Watermark* isn't a "collection of essays," of course, but rather a single long essay, originally entitled "Naberezhnaia neistselimykh"—that is, "The embankment of the incurables."

The Review *editor's introduction to the piece describes how Auden's work impressed the young Joseph Brodsky, who was then in exile in Norenskaya:"It struck an immediate chord with him and it was subsequently arranged, through intermediaries, for Auden to write an introduction to Brodsky's first book in English, launching his career in the English language."*

Of course, I would have preferred a formulation more specific than "through intermediaries." I've already told the story about how Brodsky had explicitly asked, or rather wished, for Auden to write the foreword, and how that came about.

Did you ever tell Brodsky what you thought of the elegy for Auden?

Yes. I vividly recall his first showing me that poem. I read it carefully, thought about it for a few minutes, and then said, "Joseph, perhaps there's a line or two here that are acceptable, but I'm sorry to say that your elegy simply doesn't work as an English poem." He was obviously offended and became very defensive. It was clear to me that in late 1973 his mastery of literary English was faulty and incomplete. I assume that other native speakers of English to whom he showed his elegy reacted as I did. But he went ahead and published it, first in the *Review*, and then in the 1975 volume of tributes to Auden which Spender edited.

On more than one occasion Brodsky said to me approvingly, after he had read the final version of one of my translations: "Slovar′ khoroshii" [A good lexicon]. He meant that I had used the right set of words—words that were appropriate to the sense of the poem, words that had the right *gravitas,* were at the right level of dignity or solemnity. It's curious that he failed to apply that rule to his own elegy. He somehow didn't realize that the word "fun" doesn't belong in the lexicon of an elegy:

> The tree is dark, the tree is tall,
> to gaze at it isn't fun.

It turns out that this tree is a fruit tree, an apple or pear tree, which means that it may be appropriately described as "dark," but it can hardly be described as "tall"—at least in comparison to a pine tree or oak tree. This means that the word is there primarily for the unwelcome purpose of providing a rhyme with "fall" in the subsequent line.

As you must know, Brodsky was very sensitive to the seasons of the year, especially to the coincidence of the year's beginning and a life's ending. Consider his "On the Death of T. S. Eliot" in 1965. Its first line is "On umer v ianvare, v nachale goda," which I translated as "He died at the start of year, in January." Brodsky considered it in some sense appropriate that Auden had died in late September, when fruits were ripe and falling to the ground. And Auden's death, in Brodsky's image, was "the heaviest fruit of all":

> Among the fruits of this fall
> your death is the most grievous one.

In any case, he gave Spender permission to include his "Elegy" in the volume of tributes to Auden that appeared in 1975.

You know what happened later? I'm sure you do.

Let's hear your version.

Later he said, "Oh God, I gave Spender permission to publish my poem in the volume dedicated to the memory of Auden." Joseph realized that by doing so he had "ruined an otherwise a perfectly good book." Note that he never included the elegy to Auden in any of his own collections of verse, whereas the later and much more successful elegy to Lowell, first published in the *New York Review of Books* in 1977, was reprinted in *A Part of Speech* in 1980.

Of course, he wrote the Elegy directly in English, to honor Auden and his language. He defended it against my—and I assume other people's—criticism: that it didn't work as an English poem. This was in 1973 or '74, when, as I have said, his mastery of literary English was not yet complete.

This was the same period when he approved Carl Proffer's decision to publish Jamie Fuller's "embarrassingly bad"—to quote Donald Hall—translations of some of his poems in *Russian Literature TriQuarterly*. Joseph knew enough English to recognize that Fuller had reproduced his rhymes and meters, but he didn't yet recognize the horrors, including "trite poeticisms, dead metaphors, archaisms, and vapid abstractions," which Hall immediately recognized.[4] It took a few years, at least three or four, before his literary English had become fluent enough for him to recognize what some of us had been saying from the beginning, that his elegy didn't work as an English poem, and for him to renounce it and express regret for having allowed Spender to include it in the volume of tributes to Auden.

The worst thing about the *New York Review* reprinting of this elegy is that readers will, understandably, conclude from this example, especially if they haven't seen much else, that Joseph was indeed, as that Brit declared, a "world-class mediocrity."

His relationship with translators has started to create a literature of its own. Weissbort's book From Russian with Love, *comes to mind. But there have been other accounts.*

My own relationship as translator with Joseph as author was wonderful for the first dozen or fifteen years, from roughly 1967 to 1982. Philip Clendenning, when he appraised the five cartons of mostly Brodsky related

---

4   In an October 31,1973, letter to Brodsky, Kline cites Hall's "Knock Knock" column in the January/February 1973 issue of *The American Poetry Review*. Hall had attended a September 19, 1972, Ann Arbor poetry reading, which was covered by CBS television. According to Kline's letter, APR editor Stephen Parker had suggested the translations were Fuller's, although it's not entirely certain.

material I donated to the Beinecke Library at Yale, stated that the correspondence he had sampled made it clear that ours was not only a real friendship, but also a very productive and harmonious collaboration.

You're referring to the part where he writes: "Professor Kline's active, determined and lengthy support of Brodsky immensely aided in his finding employment and income. Kline's excellent translations also made his poetry accessible to the English-speaking world and the numerous drafts and comments reflect the sincere partnership and genuine friendship between the two. This appraiser feels that without Kline's unwavering support over twenty-eight years, Brodsky's poetry and high reputation would have been considerably diminished. The value of this material reflects this marriage of poetic genius."[5]

As for that final sentence, it was Brodsky, of course, not Kline who was the "poetic genius." Otherwise, what Clendenning says about our friendship and partnership is both perceptive and true, and I give Joseph full credit. From the beginning he was always very helpful and ready to work with me, to answer my questions and clarify obscurities in his texts. I couldn't have asked for a better relationship with an author. Later the relationship began to change.

Yet even as early as 1980's A Part of Speech, *some poets, translators, readers were objecting. Robert Hass in the* New Republic *lamented his "fatal miscalculations of tone," which made him sound like one of those "clever young Englishmen of indeterminate age down from the university and set to make a splash."[6]*

Hass is inconsistent. He sharply criticized several of my lines in "Nature Morte" but went on to say that my translation of "Nunc Dimittis" was "beautiful and very simple." Similarly, with critic John Bayley. In his review of *A Part of Speech* he praised the way I had, in my "On the Death of Zhukov" translation, "miraculously managed to preserve" the slow interrupted beat of a military funeral march. In a later review, however, he said, without naming me, that the translator of the Zhukov poem had failed to convey

---

5   "Clendenning's appraisal of 'G. L. Kline's Papers,'" email from Philip Clendenning George Kline, dated April 2, 2010. Corrected version—April 22, 2010—in the Kline papers in my possession.
6   Robert Hass, "Lost in Translation," *New Republic*, Dec. 20, 1980.

either "the simplicity or the complexity" of that poem.[7] With respect to *A Part of Speech,* don't forget that Henry Gifford, the senior British Slavist, in his *TLS* review, said that "Brodsky and Kline are Brodsky's best translators"—this in a book with translations by Hecht, Walcott, and Wilbur.

The exact words: "Every poem in the book reads as if English had been its first home. Some are better than others (particularly those handled by Brodsky and by George L. Kline)."[8]

I agree with Gifford to this extent: I think that some, although not all, of Brodsky's self-translations in that book are first rate.

So when did the relationship begin to change, as you put it?

Perhaps I shouldn't have said, "began to change." Rather, it changed in the 1980s, as his mastery of literary English improved. As his mastery became more nearly complete he didn't need translators as much as he had initially. He had needed competent translators desperately in the beginning.[9]

---

7   John Bayley, "Not Afraid of Sounding Major," *New York Times*, November 27, 1988; John
    Bayley, "The Brodsky Paradox," *Los Angeles Times,* October 29, 2000. Kline's memory is
    in error, however. The later Bayley review had been the more favorable one.

8   Henry Gifford, "The Language of Loneliness," *Times Literary Supplement*, August 11,
    1978, 903.

9   Zakhar Ishov offers an even-handed account of what occurred during those years:

    One of the possible reasons that may account for Brodsky's new attitude towards Kline
    can be traced back to the dramatic change in Brodsky's own situation. At the time of
    the preparation of *Selected Poems* Brodsky was a beleaguered, persecuted poet whose
    manuscripts could not be smuggled out of the country without very high risk to all
    involved. So, while it is true that *Joseph Brodsky: Selected Poems* was the first English
    edition of Brodsky's verse over which Brodsky exercised editorial control, it is also true
    that while he remained in the Soviet Union he had very little influence over the choice of
    his translators. At that stage of his career, Brodsky was obliged to rely on a few devoted
    persons such as Kline and Proffer. Now, thanks to his newly acquired fame and respect
    in the world of American letters, in his new "reincarnation" Brodsky could count on
    participation in the translation of his verse of such prominent figures of the local
    Parnassus as Richard Wilbur, Anthony Hecht, Howard Moss, and Derek Walcott—a
    list of names, as one reviewer observed, which "read like a roll-call of an Academy of
    English-Speaking poets" (Peter Porter, "Satire with a Heart," *The Observer* [December
    14, 1980], 28). . . . Understandably, Brodsky was tempted to give precedence to the
    translators who were poets themselves, hoping at the time for a more "poetic" outcome
    from their translations, as opposed to those done by "mere" translators of poetry such
    as Kline. . . . And yet, arguably, translations done by the "real" poets—with perhaps one
    exception of "that miracle of adaptation" ("'Magic Industry' and Lachlan Mackinnon, A
    break from dullness: The virtues of Brodsky's English verse," *Times Literary Supplement*

Remember what he said when I phoned him in London after the Nobel Prize had been announced in October? I said, "Congratulations, Joseph!" and he responded "Congratulations to you too, George!" That response was justified in the sense that my translations played a role in his becoming a Nobel laureate. I wouldn't claim that they played a dominant role. But I can say, without false modesty, that they played an essential role. Without my work as translator he might eventually have won a Nobel Prize, but not as early as he did.

If you look at the table of contents of his last book of verse—what is it called, *Et Cetera?*

That's the title in some of the foreign editions. So Forth *in English. Too bad, really, "et cetera, et cetera" was one of his trademark refrains, the tail end of so many of his sentences.*

If I remember correctly, no translator is mentioned anywhere in the text of that book. In contrast, in all of his books of verse before that, following each poem, the translator would be identified. The formula was "translated by x," or in certain cases "translated by x with the author" or "translated by the author."

Anyway, in this case, one group of poems is identified on the half-title page, in small print, as "written in English," another group as "translated by the author," and those two groups include a huge majority—fifty-six poems of the sixty-four poems in this collection. Then there's the final small group of eight poems, each one of which is identified as "translated by x and the author." I'm in that group: "'An Admonition' was translated by George L. Kline and the author." There is only one poem that is identified only by the name of the translator." "'Venice: Lido' was translated by Alan Myers." Myers is the only translator, who, so to speak, gets "solo booking." In a word, the English poetry in this collection was produced by Brodsky alone, or by Brodsky with a translator. Of course, as you know, *So Forth* got slammed by most of the critics.

William Logan, writing in the New Criterion *in 2001, said that his self-translations were akin to "a barber cutting his own hair."*[10] *It was the continuation*

[June 22, 2001], 12), the translation of "Six Years Later" by Richard Wilbur—proved to be less fruitful for Brodsky in the long run. As result, *A Part of Speech* acquired the traits of what Derek Walcott described as a "not necessarily desirable variety of an anthology of Brodsky seen through the eyes of contemporary American poets" (Derek Walcott, "Magic Industry," 12).

See Ishov, "Post-horse of Civilisation," 150–51.

10   William Logan, "All Over the Map," *New Criterion* 20, no. 4 (December, 2001): 78.

of what he had written shortly after Brodsky's death: "Brodsky wrote English prose with rapacious appetite and fluency, but his poetry often sounds like verse by Humbert Humbert. You hear, as if through a lath-and-plaster wall, a noble, muffled intelligence. In his essay 'To Please a Shadow,' Brodsky claimed he wrote in English only to get closer to Auden, and some of his poems sound like Auden read through a pair of tin cans connected by string."[11]

Joseph so much wanted to honor Auden—with the elegy, with these poems. Yet Auden's sensibility was so completely foreign in temperament, training, and poetic instincts.

Remember that Brodsky had *read* Yeats, Dylan Thomas, Frost, Wilbur and Wallace Stevens, but Auden was the first English-language poet he actually *met.* He told me that, fearing to say something awkward or ungrammatical, he limited his conversation to questions of the form "Mr. Auden, what do you think of X?" or "Mr. Auden, what is your opinion of Y?" And of course Auden was happy to give the young Russian poet his view of Yeats, or Eliot, or Dylan Thomas, or Wallace Stevens.

Anyway, the attempt to translate himself brought out that mimetic longing— as Logan wrote, "reading their wayward, tone-deaf lines makes you admire Nabokov and Conrad."

Actually, I don't see why one needs to read Brodsky's flawed English stanzas to admire either Nabokov or Conrad. In any case, every other book of Brodsky's—both his collections of poems and his collections of essays—had a better reception than *So Forth.* His essays were uniformly, and justifiably, praised. And all of his other books of poetry were well received, though certain reviewers picked out a few things to criticize. Mostly the poems were in translation, whether it was mine or somebody else's. This final book of poems written in English and poems translated by Brodsky himself is the one that drew the attack of that British critic . . . you must know about it.

Craig Raine. I never found it in the Financial Times *archives. I had to get a volume of Raine's essays,* In Defense of T. S. Eliot, *to read it. The review was called "A Reputation Subject to Inflation."*

---

11   William Logan, "Old Guys," *New Criterion* 15, no. 4 (December 1996): 66.

I think this was written after Joseph's death too, which made it especially nasty. Raine called Brodsky a "world-class mediocrity." That was part of Raine's summing up. He had gone through *So Forth* and found something terribly wrong on almost every page, especially with the things Joseph had written in English or translated himself. I want to stay out of that fight as much as I can.

The last sentence of the review was pretty damning, and in the past tense, so it must have been after Brodsky's death: "He was a nervous, world-class mediocrity—bluffing but aware of his uncertain feel for the English language on which his international reputation was so precariously founded." He pretty much took him apart.

He did indeed!

Yet in this, as in so much else, he missed much about the poetry. For example, in Joseph's fortieth birthday poem "May 24, 1980," with its final two lines, as translated by Brodsky himself:

> *Yet until brown clay has been crammed down my larynx,*
> *only gratitude will be gushing from it.*

He wrote: "It is no use pointing out that burial after death seldom involves the undertaker in the task of cramming clay (of whatever complexion) down the throat of the deceased. The melodrama is entirely of Brodsky's making."[12] Raine misses the allusions to Heine, Pushkin, Mandelstam, even Tsvetaeva, and others. It redolent with the Russian poetry of the past.

As Valentina Polukhina has indicated to me, those lines very clearly echo Akhmatova's "Poem without a Hero":

> *Полумёртвая и немая,*
> *Рот её сведён и открыт,*
> *Словно рот трагической маски,*
> *Но он чёрной замазан краской*
> *И сухою землёй набит.*

---

12 Craig Raine, "A Reputation Subject to Inflation," *Financial Times*, November 16, 1996. Also in Craig Raine, *In Defence of T. S. Eliot* (London: Pan Macmillan, 2011).

Mute, half-dead,
a puckered grimace its mouth,
that could be the mouth of a tragic
mask, but for the black daub,
the stuffed-in dry earth.

(*trans. D. M. Thomas*)

Good point.

It also reminds us of Tsvetaeva's "to shut my mouth with clay" and Heine's "To Lazarus":

So we keep asking, over and over
Until a handful of earth
Stops our mouths—
But is that an answer?

That said, Raine has an interest in Russian poetry. He's married to Pasternak's niece. His wife, Ann Pasternak Slater, is the daughter of Boris Pasternak's sister.

I didn't know that. The only Pasternak I knew, not personally, but knew about, was Lydia Pasternak Slater in England, who translated some of Pasternak's poems and did a commendable job.

Ann is her daughter. I had lunch with her at their house in Oxford some time ago. Oxford has many of Leonid Pasternak's paintings and sketches. He would be her grandfather, Boris's father.

Well, that gives Raine's criticisms a certain weight. But does he himself read Russian? If he does, if he has read Brodsky's Russian poetry in the original, I can't imagine his saying that his "international reputation" was "precariously founded" on his "uncertain feel for the English language."

I understand he doesn't know Russian.

Everyone who has read Brodsky's Russian poems agrees that he is a superb poet, a poet with "absolute" pitch and impeccable literary taste. As for his self-translated poems and poems written directly in English, let me just say that Ann Kjellberg and Zak Ishov have taken up the defense of "the English Brodsky," and I trust them to make the best case that can be made. As I said, I prefer to stay out of that dispute.

Zakhar Ishov discusses this in his dissertation, which he defended at the Free University of Berlin. My only quarrel with Zak concerns a matter of chronology. He claims that in the late 1970s, for example, in the process of translating the poem I mentioned earlier, "A Second Christmas by the Shore," when Brodsky objected to my version of a given line, he himself wrote the replacement line, which we both then discussed and finally accepted. My clear memory of this period is that, on the contrary, I wrote the replacement line, which Brodsky then accepted or rejected. I also remember clearly that Brodsky's practice of supplying the replacement line himself did not begin until the 1980s, with our work on my translations of "Eclogue V: Summer" and later "An Admonition," published respectively in *To Urania* and *So Forth*.

Daniel Weissbort made an important contribution to the question of "Brodsky in English." His From Russian with Love *is an odd and meandering work, but at various points in the book he makes a very clear case that Brodsky was trying to do something with the English language that had never been done before. I wrote in the* Kenyon Review:

> *Yet despite the waffling and self-deprecation, he makes a central, remarkable contention: Weissbort argues that Brodsky "was trying to Russianize English, not respecting the genius of the English language, . . . he wanted the transfer between the languages to take place without drastic changes, this being achievable only if English itself was changed."*
>
> *In short, Weissbort invites us to listen to Brodsky's poetry on its own terms. As he tells a workshop: "It's like a new kind of music. You may not like it, may find it absurd, outrageous even, but admit, if only for the sake of argument, that this may be due to its unfamiliarity. Give it a chance, listen!"*[13]

---

13   Daniel Weissbort, *From Russian with Love* (London: Anvil, 2004), 195, 110. Cited in Cynthia L. Haven, "Uncle Grisha Was Right," *Kenyon Review* 28, no. 3 (Spring 2006): 159–68.

I guess that's the line that Ann is pursuing and perhaps Zak as well. One thing Zak told me when he first got in touch by phone and email was how much he liked my translation of "An Admonition." I'm not so sure that I like it, mainly because of the numerous changes to my draft that Joseph insisted on. Some are minor, like his putting "stinking rugs" where I had the accurate "stinking rags." I tried to correct that error, but it somehow crept back into the text as published in *So Forth*. Fortunately, with Ann's help, I was able to restore the correction in Brodsky's *Collected Works in English*. Other changes were more significant, like his adding various words solely for the sake of rhymes.

The way I put it in a recent email to the poet Irina Mashinski: "When *A Part of Speech* came out in 1980, all the collaboration up until then was fine. He never insisted against my judgment on anything."

So what happened in the 1980s?

In the 1980s and 1990s, when I was completing my translations of two long poems—"Eclogue V: Summer" and "An Admonition"—he was ready to override the judgment of his translator. He would say something like this: "We've got to return the proofs in two weeks. I've made some changes to make your version more consistent with the diction of the poems I've written in English. This will have to be the final version." A few of his changes were acceptable, but others struck me as disastrous.

From the letter he wrote from South Hadley on February 15, 1987, about your "Eclogue":

> I think we better consider this version final. I had to redo it largely because most of the translations in the forthcoming book are done by my humble self anyway, and the idea is to sustain the diction. As you'll see, a great deal of your version has survived—if not in fact, then in a somewhat restructured form. There are, of course, losses—to your version as well as to the original—but the tonality of the poem sustains them better than some of your gains that seemed to me at times a bit dangling and burdensome for its body to carry. Please, for all the sakes possible, don't be irritated, upset, dismayed and what not by that. The previous version was good by all thinkable standards, except it projected a sensibility (through its rhymes as well as through elaborations of this or that image) that would be at odds with the texture of other pieces in the collection. There is enough of you in this final version to have your name underneath it; of course we can add

'and the Author' so that one would know whom to blame for its infelicities—and
so that you knew who needs your help (right away!) in correcting them.

I believe that he did this with his other translators, as well. I've talked about translating Brodsky with Dick [Wilbur], and Danny [Weissbort], although I don't recall any discussions with them of cases where Brodsky overrode their literary judgment. The first major poem that he wrote in emigration, "1972," appears with the phrase "Translated by Alan Myers with the author." I haven't been in touch with Myers about it, but I can't imagine that he was happy with the triple dactylic rhymes of their version, most of which sound strained and awkward in English.

After my experience with "Eclogue V" and "An Admonition," I felt that collaboration with Brodsky had become impossible, and I assume that he felt that way, too. At least he didn't urge or invite me to translate anything else after that. A related point was, of course, that I didn't feel as close to the poems he was writing in that late period. Some of them I like and some had wonderful lines and stanzas, but in general I didn't feel "I've got to translate that." The exception was "The Butterfly" in 1973. When I saw that poem I thought, "I've got to translate this," just as I had with "The Elegy for John Donne" when I first encountered it in 1964.

Sometime during this period he appeared on a panel about verse translation. I wasn't there, obviously, but it was televised and someone brought that scene to my attention. And Brodsky was saying, "Well, you know it's hard to work with your translator," or maybe he put it, "It's hard to get your translator to do the right thing." "Especially," he added, "when he's older than you are." Well, that was obviously a crack at me, because I'm nineteen years older than Joseph.

Why would the age of the translator be relevant at all?

Oh, because he had an enormous respect for age.

Oh, I see.

Partly, I suspect, it was because of his deep admiration and affection for Akhmatova, who was in seventies in the 1960s, when he met her. He loved and admired her for the next six years until she died. But in this case he seemed to be saying, "Well, I might be able to control my translator if he wasn't older than I am."

He wasn't insulting me, but criticizing me for not being more pliable. For resisting his suggestions that he thought were fine, and that I thought weren't. So our harmonious collaboration came to an end.[14]

You have referred to Joseph's eventual mastery of the English language, but how much did he ever inhabit the English language—how much could he? Native speakers are picking up the nuance, the weight, the measure of words from the cradle. Conrad is the great exception, since even Nabokov had an English governess as a child, at least.

Good question. He aspired to a total mastery of literary English, but never quite attained such mastery. I've mentioned his inappropriate use of the word "fun" in 1973. But he was still using that word in a less than appropriate way in 1991. He took it in the first case to mean anything pleasant, so he expressed the idea "to gaze at it makes one feel sad or melancholy" by saying "to gaze at it isn't fun." In 1991, he used the expression "for fun" to mean "not for money." In his "Festschrift for George L. Kline," the poem he wrote for me on my retirement from teaching—while he was airborne en route from Mount Holyoke to Philadelphia—he wrote:

> He served in the US Air Force,
> Studied and taught philosophies,
> Translated me of course—
> For fun, not, alas, for colossal fees.[15]

In fact, when I translated Brodsky—and the labor was considerable—it wasn't "for fun" in the sense of for recreation any other non-serious reason. I undertook the considerable labor, as I had earlier with Pasternak and Tsvetaeva and did later with Akhmatova, out of a sense of obligation. I valued those poems, I felt competent to render them into English, and I felt that I should do my best for the sake of Russian poetry and the understanding

---

14 As Ann Kjellberg, executor for the Brodsky Estate notes, however, the two men in fact continued their collaboration, and were discussing revising and reissuing the *Selected* to the end of Brodsky's life.

15 Brodsky's lighthearted tribute is included in the occasional poems at the end of this volume.

and appreciation of that poetry by English and American readers. Again, the word "fun" violates the "good lexicon" rule, introducing a jarring note into an otherwise lovely poem.

By the way, Joseph was especially proud of the compound slant rhyme "philosophies/colossal fees."

Joseph Brodsky, George Kline, and poet Peter Viereck, a history professor at Mount Holyoke, at Memphis State University in April 1974. (Photo: John George, Memphis Press-Scimitar)

Chapter 6

Kline Takes up the Gauntlet

In the April 5, 1973, issue of the New York Review of Books, *you restated what you had told Joseph Brodsky at your first meeting: "His poetic achievement during the decade since 1962 bears comparison in my judgment with that of thirty-two-year-old Anna Akhmatova (as of 1921), the thirty-two-year-old Boris Pasternak (as of 1922), and the thirty-two-year-old Marina Tsvetayeva and Osip Mandelstam (both as of 1924)." And you went on to say that he would rank alongside them.*

A few months later, on July 19, Gleb Struve wrote in the same publication that he read your words with "the greatest imaginable surprise." He noted his own longstanding enthusiasm for Joseph Brodsky, and his role in bringing about Joseph Brodsky's first collection, Stikhotvoreniya i poemy *[Short and long poems], which was published by Inter-Language Literary Associates, with his introduction.*

Then he threw down the gauntlet: "To me—and I do not think I am alone in this—this is a ridiculously hyperbolized evaluation, and I see it as rather a disservice to Brodsky himself. Let George Kline name even a few of his poems which come up to the general level of those volumes of his then coevals."

Your answer was striking in its firmness and brevity: "I do not feel that it would be appropriate for me to respond to Mr. Struve's letter. I prefer to let Brodsky's poetry speak for itself."

Let me say something in response to some people who've questioned whether Brodsky was a great poet. Six poems certainly put him in that rank. "Elegy for John Donne." Let's see . . . well there's "Nunc Dimittis," and "The Butterfly," and then the Dante poem "December in Florence." I would

Joseph Brodsky received the Nobel award in 1987. (Photo: Leif Blom)

probably put "Conversations with an Angel" at the head of the list of the six poems. If not the first one, high on the list because it is one of the strongest. It's so rich and wonderful.

That's five, actually, but I think every serious reader will have a candidate for the sixth. And you're missing some of the late greats, "The Hawk's Cry in Autumn," and even the 1975 "Lullaby of Cape Cod," which you tried to translate.

But let's answer Gleb Struve's challenge and drill down a little deeper into some of those poems you translated, beginning with the 1963's "Elegy for John Donne," which was so important to you, not only as a magnificent poem in itself, but important in your personal history with Joseph. We'll talk about your collaboration of many of the later poems, and of course the one especially close to you, "The Butterfly."

"Elegy for John Donne"

You mentioned when you first saw the "Elegy for John Donne" it was unlike anything that was coming out of Russia at that time and I wanted to get your words on what, in particular, was different about this 1963 poem, from all the other Russian poems you were seeing then, and what impressed you.

You mean when I first saw and had a chance to look at it in Warsaw? Well, my God, it sounded like a poem by John Donne or Marvell or one of those metaphysical school poets. There's absolutely nothing political about it. The language was stately and eloquent and very moving. Especially at the end. How did that go?

> Like some great bird, he too will wake at dawn;
> but now he lies beneath a veil of white,
> while snow and sleep stitch up the throbbing void
> between his soul and his own dreaming flesh.

> (trans. George L. Kline)

I hadn't seen anything like that by any Soviet poet—any poet writing in the 1950s or '60s.

*The images of a world asleep, and the words that jump out from the pages:
"star," "snow" . . .*

Donne's stars often have religious overtones, and this one has more: it
evokes the *stelle* that ends each part of the *Divine Comedy*—the *Inferno*, the
Purgatorio, and the *Paradiso*. Especially the *Inferno*: "e quindi uscimmo a
riveder le stelle."

And sleep, and death . . . with the conventional associations between the two.

The first part of the poem is dominated by sleep and silence, the second
part with weeping. The third shorter part is dominated by dawn, and wak-
ing—and by running water, and by the star.

The poem turns on two ideas: that the poet creates a world, and that this
world dies with him. In another sense the world he creates is deathless. And
of course, Donne played with those same ideas. Also, in "The Progress of
the Soul," Donne speaks of death stringing heaven and earth together, on
the thread of the human soul. Elsewhere, the body as a garment for the soul.

Which becomes threadbare with age and approaching death.

Somewhere Donne speaks of spinning the "last thread" of his life.[1]

*You've described the falling snow becoming "snowflake needles" stitching body
to soul and earth to heaven. So much is included in this poem that was writ-
ten when he was so very young.*

It has so many allusions to Donne's work, and to his life. London is there,
and St. Paul's Cathedral, where he was dean, and his famous Island that was
England and the individual soul.

*He knew Donne's works so well—even in the Soviet Union. You once men-
tioned him being inspired by a portrait of John Donne.*

---

1 From Donne's "Hymne to God the Father": "I have a sin of fear, that when I have spun /
My last thread, I shall perish on the shore" (John Donne, *The Complete Poetry and
Selected Prose* [New York: Modern Library, 1994], 270-71).

That's true. He had heard somewhere the sort of stories about John Donne being wrapped in his funeral gear while he was alive and then lying in St. Paul's.

The winding sheet is in the poem, too!

He told me that he hadn't read much on John Donne at that point, but he had a wonderful intuitive sense what John Donne was like.

The poem shows a world shrouded in white, and the poet sees John Donne in his white shroud, as in the engraving by Martin Droeshout. He posed in his winding sheet for a portrait, to remind himself of his imminent death. According to Izaak Walton's Life of John Donne, *"In this posture he was drawn at his just height; and when the picture was fully finished, he caused it to be set by his bed-side, where it continued and became his hourly object till his death."[2] He died five weeks later.*

I assume he heard about it, but I don't really know. He did look at a lot of images as you can see, for example, in the poem "Daedalus."

Art was important to him—he was constantly sketching. Was his poem "Daedalus in Sicily" inspired by Pieter Bruegel the Elder's Landscape with the Fall of Icarus? *It's interesting that it was the same painting that had inspired Auden's "Musée des Beaux Arts." It would match Brodsky's reference to "behind, shine the tusks of the local mountains." And the poem is tagged "1993 Amsterdam," a stone's throw, so to speak, from the musée in Brussels. As if the poets were continuing their conversation together.*

Yes.

However, it wasn't just the image of Donne that inspired him. He had more than a portrait on his mind. In 1981, he did a Radio Free Europe *interview with Ukrainian writer Igor Pomerantsev that only aired in 2010, on the seventieth anniversary of Brodsky's birth.[3]*

---

2 Izaak Walton, *Izaak Walton's Lives of John Donne, Henry Wotton, Richard Hooker and John Herbert* (London: Routledge, 1888), 71.

3 All citations taken from Igor Pomerantsev, "Brodsky on Donne: 'The Poet Is Engaged in the Translation of One Thing into Another,'" Radio Free Europe/Radio Liberty, May

In the interview he specifically credits the Hemingway epigraph in For Whom the Bell Tolls *as an inspiration: "No man is an island entire of itself; every man is a piece of the continent, a part of the main; if a clod be washed away by the sea, Europe is the less, as well as if a promontory were, as well as any manner of thy friends or of thine own were; any man's death diminishes me, because I am involved in mankind. And therefore never send to know for whom the bell tolls; it tolls for thee."*

He was apparently reading For Whom the Bell Tolls *in the Soviet Union:*

Igor Pomerantsev: *Your poem "Great Elegy to John Donne" began circulating in samizdat in the Soviet Union in the mid-1960s. Donne was virtually unknown in the Soviet Union at that time. How did you discover him?*

Joseph Brodsky: *I stumbled across him the same way most people did: in the epigraph of the [Hemingway] novel* For Whom The Bell Tolls. *For some reason I felt this came from a line of verse and so I tried to find a translation of Donne. It was futile. Only later did I guess it was a fragment from a sermon. In some sense, Donne began for me the same way as he did for his English contemporaries. He was much better known in his day as a preacher than a poet.*

The most interesting aspect was how I obtained a book of his. I had searched through the anthologies. In 1964 I was given five years [sentence for social parasitism], arrested, and sent to Arkhangelsk Oblast, and for my birthday Lidiya Korneyevna Chukovskaya sent me, probably from her father's library, a "Modern Library" edition of Donne. This was when I first read all of Donne's poetry, read it seriously. . . . I wrote it, I think, in '62, when I knew remarkably little about Donne—in other words practically nothing, except a few fragments from his sermons and poems that I had found in anthologies. The main circumstance that moved me to undertake this poem was the possibility that it seemed to me existed at that period, the possibility of the centrifugal movement of a poem . . . well, not so much centrifugal . . . like a stone falling into a pond . . . and the gradual ripple outwards . . . a device more from cinematography, yes, when the camera moves back from the center.

24, 2010. Translated from the Russian by Frank Williams, and republished with the generous permission of Igor Pomerantsev.

So, in answer to your question, I would say it was more the image of the poet. Not so much the image even as the image of a body in space. Donne is English, he lives on an island. And starting with his bedroom, the perspective steadily widens. First the room, then his neighborhood, then London, the whole island, the sea, then his place in the world. At that time, this didn't so much, I would say, interest me as gripped me at the moment when I was composing it.

This brings up another point. He often credited Akhamatova for his understanding of Christianity, but surely translating Donne—who was, after all, an Anglican preacher as well as poet—had something to do with his life-long affinities with Christianity.

I'm sure some of it was Donne.

Again, "You have to remember that John Donne in his time was remembered more as a preacher than a poet and that's how I came to him."

Yes, that's good. As you note, he obviously was familiar with perhaps the most famous of Donne's sermons, "No man is an island."

Another inspiration for "Elegy": he had a major contract with the academic series Literaturnye pamiatniki [Literary monuments].

That was a little later, soon after his return from Norenskaya in 1965. He had a contract to translate 4,000 lines of the poetry of the metaphysical poets for this Soviet publisher. He was translating Donne, Marvell, and others into Russian, while writing his own poetry as well. He was very enthusiastic about it. Of course he'd only done, I don't know, a couple hundred lines, I guess, and never continued.

A shame. Tell me a little more about that project.

Thanks to the literary historian Viktor Zhirmunsky, he had a contract with a Soviet publisher that paid ninety kopeks a line for a 4,000-line volume of the English metaphysical poets. The total would have been a total of 3,600 rubles. But he wasn't to receive the money until he delivered the manuscript, which he never did, and which, in any case may have taken years. I think we should say something about Brodsky as translator, especially of English poetry. He was a superb translator.

Clearly, the translations he did taught him a good deal about Donne. The Pomerantsev interview speaks to that, too:

> **Pomerantsev**: *You've translated several of Donne's poems. They say a translator is always in competition with the author he translates. How did you feel translating Donne—like a competitor, ally, pupil, or colleague?*
>
> **Brodsky**: *Well, absolutely not as a competitor. Competition with Donne is absolutely out of the question thanks to Donne's qualities as a poet. He is one of the greatest figures in world literature. . . . A translator, simply a translator, not an ally. . . . Perhaps more of an ally, since a translator is always to some extent an ally. A pupil, yes, because I learned an awful lot by translating him.*
>
> *The thing is that Russian poetry is overwhelmingly strophic; that is, it operates through extraordinarily simple strophic units—four-line stanzas. While in Donne's verse I encountered a much more interesting and thrilling structure. He creates extraordinarily complex strophic constructions. I found it very interesting, and very instructive. So, consciously or unconsciously, I began doing the same but not as a competitor—as a pupil. That was probably the main lesson. And then again, when you read or translate Donne you learn from his view of things. What I really liked about Donne was the translation of the heavenly to the earthly—i.e., the translation of the eternal to the transient.*

I'm told that the Russian reader is struck by the urgent, modern language of the poem. When you translated the "Elegy for John Donne," however, were you were trying to recreate a modified seventeenth-century diction?

In the first 1965 blank verse rendering of the John Donne poem, I translated *ty* and *tvoi* as "thou" and "thy" or "thine." This usage seemed to me to suggest the spirit and time of Donne. When I sent it to Joseph later, he responded enthusiastically, adding "Chort s nimi, s rifmami, esli poluchaetsia tak." [To hell with those rhymes! What happens, happens.]

That was certainly an uncharacteristic reaction!

Do you know the name Viktor Frank? He was a journalist, a serious one, and also the son of a major Russian philosopher, Semyon Frank, whose widow I once met in England. I've written about his work. He said some very complimentary things, too. He apparently wasn't bothered by "thou" or "thy," So the first version was published in the *TriQuarterly Review.*

But others, including A. Alvarez, the poetry consultant for Penguin Books, persuaded me to drop it for the Penguin edition and the *Russian Review.*

I'd like to start soon on revisions for the *Selected Poems,* and I'd begin with the "Elegy for John Donne." I have a rhymed version by Andrey Navrozov and the 1968 "adaptation" of Rose Styron, which, for some reasons, stops fifty-seven lines short of the end. I've looked only briefly at the Navrozov version, but find it burdened by excessive "padding," by which I mean the use of English words or expressions that have no counterpart in the Russian text. Some of his feminine *nepolnye rifmy,* that is, inexact rhymes, are acceptable, for example, "carcass/darkness," "adjacent/embracing." Most of his masculine rhymes strike me as overused and worn out. I'll be interested in your reaction.

Irina Mashinski and I now are going over all those translations and we are probably going to make some changes. Irina was the co-winner of the Brodsky/Spender Prize. I've never met her. I guess I've told you that. I don't recall if we've even talked on the phone. We've just exchanged a bundle of emails and letters.

Let's conclude our discussion of this elegy with Joseph's words on this poem. He makes a case for Donne as a poet who anticipates our times in this passage. It continues his thought about "the translation of the eternal to the transient":

> **Brodsky**: *It's quite interesting, because there's an awful lot to be said about this. In fact, it's like Tsvetaeva said: "The voice of heavenly truth against earthly truth." Except it isn't so much "against" as the translation of heavenly truth into the language of earthly truth, i.e. of eternal phenomena into transient language. And both win as a result. It is merely the bringing nearer . . . how to put it . . . the expression of the seraphic order. Once it is spoken of, the seraphic order becomes more real. And this wonderful interaction is actually the essence, the bread of poetry.*

> *And for him there was no such thing as antagonism. I mean that antagonism for him existed as an expression of antagonism generally, in the world, in nature, but not as a specific antagonism. . . . There's so much that could be said about him. As a poet, he was fairly uneven stylistically. Coleridge said something remarkable about him. He said that when you read Donne's successors, the poets of around a century later, Dryden, Pope, and so on, everything comes down to counting syllables and feet, while reading Donne you measure not the number of syllables but time. That's exactly what Donne was doing in his verse. It's akin to Mandelstam's drawing out the caesura, yes, holding back an instant, stopping . . . for something which seems wonderful to the poet for one or another reason. Or the other way around, like in his* Voronezh Notebooks, *there you have unevenness, jumps, and truncated feet, truncated meter, feverish haste—so as to hasten or eliminate the instant which seems terrible.*

> **Pomerantsev**: *And yet the poets of the twenties and thirties, like Eliot, managed to see in Donne . . .*

> **Brodsky**: *Yes?*

> **Pomerantsev**: *. . . the spirit of their time.*

> **Brodsky**: *Certainly. Because Donne, with the themes that he raised, with his uncertainty, with the fragmentation or duality of his consciousness is, of course, a poet of our times. The problems he raises are those of mankind as a whole, and especially of man living at a time of excess information, population . . .*

It's hard to overstate the importance of this poem. The Lithuanian poet Tomas Venclova remembers first coming across Joseph's poems on the day Pasternak died, May 30, 1960, and reflecting years later, "Brodsky's 'Christmas Romance' and 'Elegy to John Donne' were magnificent works that struck a totally new note in Russian poetry—in the case of 'Elegy,' I would even say, in world poetry."[4]

He remembered the Russian's visits to Lithuania: "On every visit to Vilnius—there were at least ten of them—Joseph brought new work, which he generously shared with us. Once, he read us his translations from John Donne including 'The Flea' and 'The Storm.' Our knowledge of Donne at that time was very limited (well, everybody could recite by heart his famous lines about

---

4   Ellen Hinsey, *Magnetic North: Conversations with Tomas Venclova* (Rochester: University of Rochester Press: 2017), 245.

the tolling of the bell, taken as the title of Hemingway's novel). Therefore, the translations simply overwhelmed us. He also supplied us with English poetry books: in my diary, I noted that he gave me a large volume of Wallace Stevens and a book of Cavafy in translation (he was very fond of Cavafy, and I fell in love with him as well—soon, I translated 'Thermopylae,' 'Ithaka,' and several other poems into Lithuanian)."5

"Nunc Dimittis"

Let's move to another of the early poems you translated—a major one. Tomas Venclova says it's the most Christian and the most Akhmatovian of Brodsky's poems. That's one reason among many that the poem was important to you—to both of us.

With his 1972 poem "Nunc Dimittis," he bridges both the Old and New Testaments.

He dies, as he had been foretold, as soon as he has seen the Christ child—so in that sense, his death is the "first Christian death in history." With the central figure of St. Simeon, this poem represents a point of transition between the Old Testament and the New. "He moved and grew smaller, in size and in meaning"—it signifies that the Old Testament is fading away as the world of the New Testament is born.

The idea that the passage of time causes some historical figure to grow and others to shrink is an idea that occurs in another of his poems, "Presepio." Here it is Old Testament that must shrink, as the New Testament opens up. In "Presepio," it's Christ who grows in cosmic and historical dimensions, from his birth in the Bethlehem manger. Both these poems—all the "Nativity Poems," really—are filled with veneration for the divine, and a powerful sense of what Rudolf Otto called the *mysterium tremendum* of the holy.

Mysterium fascinans—alluring and magnetic—as well. Another transition comes to mind in the poem—from life to death, from mortality to eternity.

Simeon dies with a clear and calm awareness of what is happening to him, after a long life waiting, a life that, as Brodsky said, has become a sort of punishment to him.

---

5   Ibid., 237.

And it's also a movement from darkness to light—from the darkness of the temple interior to the shaft of light that falls on the infant. As Joseph pointed out, even as a baby he functions as a source of light—the sleeping baby blowing "drowsy bubbles" lights up what had previously been hidden in darkness, in non-being:

> And Simeon's soul held the form of the Child—
> its feathery crown now enveloped in glory—
>> aloft, like a torch, pressing back the black shadows,

Like the "Elegy for John Donne," this poem had a painting as inspiration.

It turns out he'd seen a certain painting by . . . who was it? Rembrandt's *Presentation of Jesus in the Temple.*

The painting has many vertiginous aspects, constantly pulling the eye upwards. Certainly, it's a poem that is vertical. *He was an avid reader of Pasternak, of course, and it's rather like Pasternak's poem "Christmas Star."*

> *For a while they stood whispering there in the shadows,*
> *but found little to say, until one of them felt*
> *a hand nudging him forward. He looked up and saw*
> *in the doorway, not far*
> *from him, gazing at Mary, like some special guest,*
> *the Nativity star.*
>
> (trans. Peter Oram)

Certainly the verticality shows in Brodsky's composition—the small group huddled together against those vertical columns, which send the viewer's eye upwards: "Its lofty vaults stooped as though trying to cloak . . . ," "his echoing words grazed the rafters," "high over their heads in the tall temple's vaults."

Think of the rest of the next line after the high temple's vault: "like some soaring bird that flies constantly upward."[6] The repeated "word," in both singular and plural forms, and "bird" are connected.

---

6   Occasionally, as here, Kline cites an earlier version of a line in the translated poem.

As Joseph observed, Simeon's words fly upward, like a prayer to God. And the words of a private man having a shattering encounter become universal, repeated daily by thousands the world over: "Now, o Lord, lettest thou thy poor servant, / according to thy word, leave in peace."

And the vertical ray of light in the temple is a "Rembrandtian" move, as Brodsky has said.

A haunting biographical note in this poem: "like some soaring bird that flies constantly upward/and somehow is caught and cannot return earthward." It seems to prefigure the ending of "The Hawk's Cry in Autumn," which always seemed to me to describe the poet himself, with that fatal heart as he pushed it, and pushed it.

The poem also has resonances with his other poems as well, before and after. I think again of "Gorbunov and Gorchakov," written between 1965 and '68, in which he also links life and speech, and death and silence and non-speech. "Life is but talk hurled in the face of silence."

But for him, remember, the concern with growing old and growing silent isn't only a function of biological age, of course—it's also the finality and irreversibility of his banishment from his country, his culture, and his language. Especially at the time he wrote this poem.

Space, an ongoing theme for him, figures in this poem: "he strode through the cold empty space of the temple."

And later, at the end, as Simeon departs: "He strode through a space that was no longer solid."

And the senses, even when what they are perceiving is an absence of sense.

"The roaring of time ebbed away in his ears."

"A thick silence engulfed them,/and only his echoing words grazed the rafters." Joseph noted that it's not only a silence in the face of eternity, but a confrontation with our mortality. As he said, "as the body grows older it fills up with silence—with organs and functions which are no longer relevant to its life."

Again, it echoes his poem "1972," where he spoke about "growing old," and the dulling of the "organ of hearing," which prepares it for silence.

We spoke earlier of the influence of art on Brodsky. Candlemas has been portrayed by a number of painters, including Carpaccio, Bellini, Cima da Conegliano, and others. But Brodsky himself claimed that Rembrandt's Simeon in the Temple, *which he had only seen in reproductions, was a big influence. It's an up-close and personal version of the "Presentation," and for that reason, perhaps, more like an icon.*

Yet Joseph disappears from this poem—he's not mentioned at all, in the very setting where he should be pivotal. The other Joseph, the poet Brodsky, once wanted to make an anthology of Russian poems devoted to Biblical themes, and illustrate it with images of icons—but realized his own "Nunc Dimittis" wouldn't have a place in it!

I suggested he find a special Brodsky icon—one that doesn't show Joseph!

Although, as Venclova points out, the presence of the Biblical Joseph is implied because his p.o.v. determines the narrative, before the poem shifts to the point of view of the two women, and finally, to Simeon's internal perspective, and his death "from the inside." Luke doesn't describe Joseph's perspective and only mentions his presence.

Finally, let's discuss those repetitions in "Nunc Dimittis." Joseph pointed out that the stylistic difference between the Old Testament and the New is its use of repetitions, which introduce a sort of absurdist tone. They also amplify the words semantically, making them larger in meaning with repetition.

They occur in the first lines of the poem:

> Когда она в церковь впервые внесла
> дитя, находились внутри из числа
> людей, находившихся там постоянно . . .

(When she first brought to the church / the child, inside were found, of the number / of people who were found there always. . . .) Also,

А было поведано старцу сему

о том, что увидит он смертную тьму

не прежде, чем сына увидит Господня . . .

(It had been revealed to this old man / that he would not see the darkness of death / before seeing the son of God. . . .)

And there is also the repetition of themes, here and elsewhere.

One of his central themes is the Judeo-Christian tradition, and the word "God," *Bog, Gospod'*—Lord, Lord—the word *mladenca*, baby or infant, which can mean Christ child, though I'm not quite sure it does that here, because "Nunc Dimittis" isn't a Christmas poem. It's more like an Easter poem.

But there's no Good Friday till "Nature Morte" and "Conversation with an Angel."

He uses Good Friday, but it's a Russian equivalent, which is *Strastnaia*. It means "Passionate Friday," with the implication of "terrible." So it's Passion Friday. It's a much better way to describe it than say, Good Friday. Wouldn't you agree?

Yes. The word in Russian has connotations of "terror"—which certainly was present in the original event. The word "terrible" in today's English has lost its "terror."

Anyway, what else? The whole idea from "Sreten'e," or "Nunc Dimittis," is about the beginning and the end of life, the Christ child and St. Simeon, who dies in the poem. "He went forth to die."

As with another poem "Conversation with an Angel," which ends with a howling infant, and an old man about to die.

Two unnamed people. One is *mladenets*, a Christ child or maybe just a child. I'm really not sure. Do you recall when his son Andrei was born, which year?

It was 1967, several years before this poem.

There are six religious themes in Joseph's poetry, and "Nunc Dimittis" combines several of them. The Nativity is one, the theme of suffering and sacrifice is another. Then there is the transition from the Old Testament to the New. The Easter theme. The theme of religion and modern, secular culture. And the theme of the loss or absence of a miracle.

Also, the theme of the ark, the word *kovcheg*, ark, is used and again, same theme is in "Fontan" in Russian, which was a few years earlier—"The Fountain." Remember the end of "The Fountain"? I forget the exact lines.

Like this, in your translation . . .

> *For no loneliness is deeper than the memory of miracles.*
> *Thus, former inmates return to their prisons,*
> *and doves to the Ark.*

So the doves return to the ark and prisoners return to their cells. The ark and the birds. It's all so rich. It just goes on and on. It's endless.

"Conversation with an Angel"

Let's pick up our discussion of one poem you never got around to translating, "Razgovor s nebozhitelem"—sometimes called "Conversation with an Angel," or "Conversation with a Celestial," at other times "Conversation with a Heaven-Dweller."

Listen, I'm just bubbling. I'm glowing. I went back yesterday to read that wonderful poem. It is a glorious thing.

That's another poem about "heavenly truth," as Tsvetaeva explained it—but that poem isn't widely available in English to date, though you had hoped to translate it once, I believe.

It is an absolutely splendid poem. It's as good as "The Butterfly," and it was written in the 1970s, while he was still in Russia. Have you found it somewhere?

Technically, it's a tour de force. I hadn't noticed this before, and I don't know whether a translator could do it justice, but the first sentence in the poem—guess how many lines long it is?

I'm not going to try. Six, seven.

[Laughing.] I'm laughing because it's three stanzas of eight lines—twenty-four altogether!

Twenty-four lines.

There's no comma, there's no capital letter to start a new sentence in that whole thing. Of course, six of those lines are very short. Short lines centered on the page. It has a kind of butterfly appearance, or whatever you want to call it—like "The Butterfly."

That's just really an astonishing structure for the poem. And it's impossible to render all this. I don't know what you'd do with it.

I finally got the only English translation that has appeared, in New American and Canadian Poetry *in April 1972. The translation is by William Chalsma, and a poet I hadn't heard of—Harvey Feinberg, "assisted" by a H. W. Tjalsma. Presumably Feinberg's role was poet and Chalsma or Tjalsma was the translator. It was published in* New American and Canadian Poetry *in April 1972. Chalsma . . . Tjalsma . . . the same name?*

During most of his career, he spelled it one way, but at some point he went back to his family spelling from his grandparents, or whatever. It's the same name.

I had somewhere a literal prose version. I'll try to find it.

The results in English are disappointing.

It's in free verse and it's terrible? Is that what you're saying?

That's one way of putting it. It doesn't sound like a Brodsky poem, and nothing of the magic. It's the kind of free verse trot you complain of, which found its way into publication. Moreover, the first verse translates "breviary" as "dictionary."

It's a wonderful poem in the original. Joseph said the content was basically okay, but of course he hated the fact that it was sprawling and formless, and so on.

Sprawling and formless was part of it. Did Joseph approve it?

Of course he hated the idea that his very strict form is lost. In Russian, it's exactly the form of "The Butterfly."

Joseph had approved it, as I recall. I don't believe it's in writing anywhere, but he had approved the content. The content was accurate enough, but of course he hated the form. It was totally formless.

It's exactly the same form as "The Butterfly." The same short lines, centered on the page, except it is somewhat longer. It's a glorious poem, and if I had the energy . . . I probably don't, but possibly . . . I haven't asked her yet but Irina Mashinski might be willing to collaborate with me on it. She writes very good poetry in both Russian and English.

I had to find a copy through the services of Stanford Libraries, so it's not widely available. A blessing and a shame, at once.

I gave a Brodsky seminar in Russian, I guess it was for a full year in 1988, '89, something like that. Fortunately and interestingly, I included "Conversations with an Angel" in the coursework. There weren't many students, but they were very committed and enthusiastic, and good, clever, and informed. They read it, and I'm sure we discussed it. I considered it a major work, certainly.

Some Russian friends showed it to me, and I wanted to see it translated. I don't remember how I ran across it. It must have been the Russian, but . . .

If you are in touch with Ann, encourage her to answer me because I want to know if she has any poems that are decent English poems of any of the poems that fall into that period, and of course in particular of this one.

We want to plan for the new edition of the *Selected*. She is all for it. She probably wishes I had done it some time ago. I hope I have time to do it now.

As I mentioned, the title of the poem has many variants in English: not only "Conversation with an Angel," but "Conversation with Celestial" and "Conversation with a Heaven-Dweller."

No, the Russian word *nebozhitel'* is not "being," it literally means "dweller in heaven." I don't like to translate it that way because it seems to be clear from the context that it's an angel.

He actually used the word *angel*, "angel," at one point in it—"I won't expect your answers, Angel, since . . ."

Не стану ждать
твоих ответов, Ангел, поелику

Interesting. Bethea calls it "Conversation with a Heaven-Dweller," which I suppose is more theologically accurate.

Someone who lives in heaven. I've seen it translated "celestial being," so I'm sure that's the same one. You said Tomas Venclova mentioned it. What did he say?

He wrote to me on January 15, 2013: "'Conversation with a Celestial' is an absolutely magnificent poem—I believe it was translated into English by a student of Carl Proffer just before Joseph's emigration, though I may be wrong." He mentioned it in passing.

The book you have, *Trudy i dni*, with that beautiful photo of Joseph looking out from the cover in his cap, that was taken in Venice—

The 1998 Works and Days, *edited by Pyotr Vail and Lev Losev.*

There's a chapter in it by Alexander Kushner called "Zdes', na zemle," from the first line of the poem "Here, on the earth . . ." The whole chapter is about what a great poem it is, and how it's the best thing Brodsky's ever done. It goes on and on like that. It's great.

Well, let me just go over the last lines with you because, in a sense, it's the key. Someone pointed out that happens in Brodsky's long poems. His poems, in the typical Brodsky way, are about a hundred to a hundred and fifty lines. It happens in "John Donne," it happens in "The Conversation with an Angel." The last few lines are, not only powerful, but extraordinarily moving.

I want that poem so much. From the moment I discovered this poem, I wanted to see it translated.

I know, dear. I think I memorized it. If Irina and I can last. . . . Well she can last, but if I can last long enough to translate it, it would be a real service. It ends with an old man. The poem is about the beginning of life and the end of life and it goes like this:

он видит снег и знает, что умрет
     до таянья его, до ледохода.

That's something like:

He sees the snow and knows that he will die
before the snow melts, before the ice breaks.

An old man in the hospital sees the snow. He knows that he will die before it melts, before the ice breaks up. Actually *do ledokhoda* is a key word in several other Brodsky poems. It has to do with praying and life and renewal. And it literally means movement of the ice. The ice was fixed and static all winter and when it begins to melt it begins to move. We say break up, but it's certainly the moving of the ice. The moving of the ice is a kind of precursor and symbol of the moving of life and rebirth in the spring.

Irina Mashinski described this in an email:

Ледоход (ledokhod), *ice-breaking and subsequently moving, is a phenomenon and an image (and therefore a metaphor, too) absolutely ubiquitous in Russian folklore and culture, in general. This is such an incomparable, powerful feeling—to hear the sound of ice cracking, often in the middle of the night, in the thick layer of ice, say, in Siberia, on a huge river flowing northward, to the Arctic Ocean—or in the far North—ice cracking, breaking and slowly moving in big chunks and sheets, thus signifying the beginning of spring on so many a level (at least one hopes so). For inmates, especially in the Far East, it meant reconnection with the "mainland": boat trips resuming—a possibility to leave the place of captivity or exile for those released, the prospect of an influx of letters and parcels from the family, and so on. Though Brodsky's exile was in the European North of Russia, not in Siberia or Far East, it still must have had that additional significance, as it did for the local residents of that region.*

Yes. It's really a fantastic poem.

You wrote once that, "Poetry, for Brodsky, is a revelation of 'what time does to the existing individual'—as manifested in loss, separation, deformity, madness, old age, and death. Yet it is poetry which offers a way, in the end perhaps the only *way, of enduring these horrors."*

Where did I write that?

You wrote in the 1988 Dictionary of Literary Biography, *in the entry for Joseph Brodsky. Pretty good, yes? Will we ever see this poem in an English that's true to the spirit and form of the original?*

Fortunately, "Conversation with an Angel" is not impossible. It's difficult. It's very damned difficult. I told you how many hours I guessed that I spent on "The Butterfly." Anyone who ever does it decently, it'll be that many hours, 200 or 300. Yeah, who has that to spare, on the "Conversation"?

"With a View of the Sea"

Glyn Maxwell and your friend Zakhar Ishov translated "With a View of the Sea," which was published in The New York Review of Books *on April 25, 2013, during that same poetry month we discussed earlier—but this time they're featuring a very early poem, from 1969.*

I think they'll be publishing more this week.

I've read and reread both the Russian text and the Maxwell-Ishov translation and have a mixed reaction. On the one hand, the translation conveys much of the wit and light-heartedness of the original.

That's why I rather like it. And you told Zak how much you liked it!

Joseph Brodsky shakes hands with the Sture Allén, the permanent secretary of the Swedish Academy at the Nobel ceremonies. (Photo: Leif Blom)

Yes. But many words are omitted in the translation; many others are added. In both cases this is primarily for the sake of rhyme or meter. There are a very few worn-out, cliché rhymes (such as hand/stand); almost all are slant rhymes, some quite striking (e.g., canter/[ole]ander, swarm/yawn). The translation reverses and increases the proportion of strict to slant rhymes in the original. I haven't done a count, but would estimate the proportion of strict to slant rhymes in the Russian at about nine to one. By the way, I'm not condemning this reversal. I've done this sort of thing myself, for example, in "The Butterfly," though not so one-sidedly.

In a few cases, it seems to me, "revision for the sake of rhyme and meter" goes too far. For example, in section VI, Joseph has "Pust' Vremia vziatok ne berët / Prostranstvo, drug, srebroliubivo" [Okay, Time doesn't take bribes / but Space, my friend, is money-mad]. The last word, literally "silver-loving," is an obsolete term for what the *Oxford Russian Dictionary* calls "money-grubbing." I don't think this is adequately conveyed by the lines in this translation: "Time just sniggers at / your bribe, but Space is hungry."

In the February 25, 2013, issue of the New Yorker, *another poem "In Villages God Does Not Live in Corners." Also translated by Glyn Maxwell, this time with Catherine Ciepiela.*

My first reaction to this version was that I couldn't see any improvement over the one I did, included in *Selected Poems. Po uglam* in the context of a village cottage, means "in icon corners." And I don't much like either "jigs and bops" or "potshots."

No, I don't see the *New Yorker* regularly, and am glad to be alerted to such as this translation. Ann told me when she was editing *Nativity Poems* that Maxwell was a fine poet and translator. I wasn't convinced by his version of "Christmas Ballad," though it was rhymed, which mine wasn't.

As an aside, much has been made of Joseph's affinity with art.[7] We've talked about that vis-à-vis several of the poems, especially "Nunc Dimittis." But his affinity with music was strong, too. And also architecture.

Yes, that's a very interesting point and of course he loved Venice for all those reasons.

He loved Saint Petersburg for all those reasons.

Yes, exactly.

---

7   Cf. Cynthia L. Haven, "Brodsky and His Muses," *The Hoover Digest*, July 7, 2017, 188–99.

Chapter 7

A Lullaby, a Butterfly, and an Untranslatable Poem

"1972"

Are there any poems you consider "untranslatable"?

"1972 god," or "The Year 1972," is a powerful and original poem, but one that is, strictly, untranslatable—mainly because of the triple dactylic "destructive" rhymes. Dactylic rhymes work only in light verse in English, though serious Russian poetry often uses them.[1] Moreover, the semantic "slide" or "destruction" of the triple rhymes is impossible to reproduce in English.

If I understand you properly, you are talking about inexact "rasshatannye" dactylic rhymes. The closest word in English would be "rickety"—that is, the same word one would use to refer to a chair that's old and shaky. At least, that's what your friend Irina Mashinski tells me. She writes in her email about this poem:

> *The semantic slide Kline is referring to is made possible by the very nature of dactylic rickety (rasshatannye, as Gasparov and others called them) rhymes, that is, rhymes in which the stress is on the third syllable counting from the end of the line, and the last two unstressed syllables do not rhyme exactly, but rather echo, more or less closely. This rhyming—or chiming—is deep: its "roots,"*

---

1   George Kline's chart of the "destructive" triple dactylic rhymes in the poem "1972" is on page 135.

so to speak, grow deep into the body of the line. It is also important that triple rasshatannye *rhymes have a swaying effect, partly due to the rhyming scheme adopted by Brodsky in "1972": aaabcccb.*

In English, such rhymes often have a comic, or a rap-like, effect, especially, if they are consistent throughout a poem. In Russian, though, this is all much more nuanced. And in case of repeating dactylic rhymes—say, in triples, like here—by gradually changing consonants in these last two syllables, one moves farther and farther away from the first line—hence, a slide in a chosen direction.

Whew! That's a lot to take in.

English simply doesn't have that many long rhymes. Igor Pomerantsev, we spoke of him earlier in our discussion of the "Elegy for John Donne," spoke of this. As he explained in a conversation that was later published as an interview, each language has its own "nervous system," so to speak. "Words can be translated, but the nervous system cannot be translated." The genius of Russian, its originality, is the tension between permitted literature and unauthorized literature. It's been this way since Ivan the Terrible—a constant tension between the poet and the tsar. It's not an issue in English, at least not a permanent, abiding concern under the skin of the culture. "You can transplant a heart, perhaps you can transplant a brain, but it's impossible to transplant the nervous system."

"Now about English poems," he continued. "I carefully read, sniff. What's the essence, what kind of nervous system? I think it's this confrontation between Anglo-Saxon and Latin roots. Because forty percent of English vocabulary has Latin roots, through the Normans, and almost all abstract concepts are Latin. But the earthly, objective, tangible is the Anglo-Saxon one."[2]

I'm not so sure how he figures forty percent, but certainly our most powerful rhymes tend to be Anglo-Saxon ones, not Latinate ones. Our double and triple rhymes tend to be a "reach," a Gilbert and Sullivan flavor—hence the comic effect in English.

Right. They are used to great comic effect in, say, the light verse of Ogden Nash. Examples: clammily/family, supercilious/bilious, mentally/dentally. Or the compound dactylic rhymes—Timbuctu/hymnbook too, Amazon/pajamas on, environment/Byron meant, definite/chef in it.

---

2   Ivan Tolstoy, "Poniaten li Osip Mandel'shtam inostrantsu? Beseda s Igorem Pomerantsevym," *Svoboda*, January 12, 2016. Translation mine.

Humor is the last thing different peoples seem to understand about each other.

It could be.

We've discussed this poem earlier, and you've discussed your dismay at the translation by Alan Myers and of course Joseph.

Alan Myers once claimed that there "wasn't much interaction (or cooperation)" between Joseph and himself. My suspicion is that Alan avoided the disastrous dactylic rhymes that got into the published version, and Joseph introduced some or all of them.

He wrote to Daniel Weissbort on August, 17, 1996, "Joseph and I never collaborated in the real sense":

> *My own versions were usually too smooth, light and regular ("cute") for his taste, and often prompted him to set about actually re-writing his verse, working back from a bolder, more jaggedly energetic English rhyme. The line-length, (my) rhythm, even the meaning might all undergo change. Indeed, on one occasion, he went so far as to say that* everything *should be sacrificed to the rhyme! For a sharp increase in energy level, 'smoothness' was well lost. My role became that of a provider of what Russians call* polufabrikat—*a useful three-quarter finished product for Joseph to work on. Economic considerations eventually put a stop to that. As we know, producing rhymed poetry translations takes too long to permit one to earn a living at the same time. It is the ideal prison occupation.*[3]

> *After 1980, Myers had very little to do with his poetry, though he occasionally did "raw" versions for Joseph to rework. "One about Washington and one about Venice appeared in the* TLS, *the former mostly his, the latter mostly mine. 'The Hawk's Cry' and 'Fifth Anniversary,' which are in* Urania, *were similarly produced. The former has quite a lot of my material in it, the latter not much." But Joseph was already reworking the versions for* A Part of Speech.

> *Myers notes that the plural "carps" in "Three Knights" is evidence that he wasn't consulted about final versions, and Brodsky also reworked the ending*

---

3   All citations from the Daniel Weissbort papers in Valentina Polukhina's possession. Used with permission.

of "Stone Villages." *Myers was a friend, happy to help out, and didn't object.* *"My own reputation wasn't at stake because I didn't have one." Joseph would chuckle and say to Alan, "I've been mangling your masterpieces."*

He elaborated in letter a month later, on September 5:

> *Joseph had an enormous samizdat reputation and an overwhelming and wholly justified belief in his poetic talent in his own language. After his departure from the USSR, he was faced with the crucial task of establishing a similar reputation in English. In the process, I have no doubt that he was prepared to set aside the conventions of translator-author transactions—nor did he see such transactions as dealings between equals, at least not in my case. He once said in an interview that translating poetry was like doing a crossword puzzle. He added that he felt his own rhymes were rather more enterprising than those of the natives, whose ear might be dulled by familiarity. This attitude applied to poetry only. Later on, in the plays and essays that I did, he altered very little, though he might insert afterthoughts and qualifications.*

Joseph—and I guess it was Alan Myers, poor Alan Myers—did it but that exemplifies what you're talking about: terrible, unworkable slant rhymes and compound rhymes. You remember? It doesn't come through. It's a wonderful, powerful poem in Russian. It doesn't come through in English, in my judgment.

I guess, in a way, I blame Alan for yielding. There are so many things that don't deserve all the criticism of that Englishman.

You mean Craig Raine.

Lev Loseff points out that not only are the dactylic rhymes difficult, but also the many internal references to such writers as Olesha, Mandelstam, Pushkin, Soloviev, and even the Russian-Asian Lay of Igor's Campaign—and *Plato, too, for that matter.*[4] *Stanza ten begins with "Slushai, druzhina, vragi i bratie" (Listen, my boon brethren and my enemy)—a direct reference to the* Lay of Igor's Campaign, *his address to his soldiers* (Slovo o polku Igoreve).

"1972" is full of folklore and ancient Russian history—drinking the ocean from Igor's helmet.

---

4   Lev Loseff, Стихотворения и поэмы (Saint Petersburg: Vita Nova, 2011), 576.

"Ivan's queen in her tower."

I remember how it begins in Russian: "Ptitsa uzhe ne vletaet v fortochku." "Birds don't fly through my skylight nowadays." And by the way, they're all dactylic rhymes. They work in Russian. It's almost impossible to make them work in a serious poem in English. I've written something about this.

And it's 1972. This is one of the first poems after he is kicked out of the USSR—

The first major one, yes. The first long one.

Lev Loseff says the first nine stanzas were written in Russia, and only the last seven in the first two years after his expulsion. It's almost an act of defiance, isn't it?

Defiance of the Soviets?

Yes, and the last seven stanzas deliver a punch. A way of saying "You didn't break me."

Oh sure! A way of saying, "I can still write fantastic poems." I'm sure he thought about it a lot.

And a way of signaling his devotion to the language. That tenth stanza again, in the Myers-Brodsky translation:

> What I've done, I've done not for fame or memories
> in this era of radio waves and cinemas,
> but for the sake of my native tongue and letters.

That ill-advised letter to Brezhnev—so many different versions of it exist:

> Dear Leonid Ilich: I belong to the Russian culture. I feel a part of it, a component of it, and no change of place can influence the final consequence of this. A language is a much more ancient and inevitable thing than a state. I belong to the Russian language. As to the state, from my point of view, the measure of a writer's patriotism is not oaths from a high platform, but how he writes in the language of the people among whom he lives. . . . Although I am losing

my Soviet citizenship, I do not cease to be a Russian poet. I believe that I will return. Poets always return in flesh or on paper.[5]

It's painful for me to leave Russia. I was born here, live here, and owe to it everything I have."[6]

Even the metrical form that he chose for this poem, and the "destructive" rhymes we discussed earlier, sign that and confirm it.

Maybe I discussed it with him—that he wanted to do something really striking. He did. Nobody ever did triple dactylic destructive rhymes. Almost all are slant rhymes, many of them are compound slants. And I think, by the way—I suppose you should talk to a native speaker about this—but my sense is they all work beautifully in Russian. Nothing that we consider clunky, awkward, or inappropriate. And I'm afraid almost everything in the translation is clunky.

Here is the last one anyway, the thirteenth stanza:

Данная песня—не вопль отчаянья.
Это—следствие одичания.
Это—точней—первый крик молчания,

In Alan or Joseph's translation:

This song isn't the desperate howl of deep distress.
It's the species' trip back to the wilderness.
It's, more aptly, the first cry of speechlessness,

I see what you mean about the triple dactylic rhymes. The Russian language is so flexible in its suffixes and prefixes, without any fixed word order. As Leon Aron writes in his Wall Street Journal *piece: "Without a fixed word order, auxiliary verbs such as 'is' or 'are' or articles, Russian offers little to impede the lyrical poet, and Brodsky rejoiced in this paradigmatically inflected language. Rich shades of emotions and meanings are conveyed by prefixes and suffixes. Myriad rhymes are generated almost spontaneously as the mostly*

---

5   There are various versions of this letter, and of course various translations. This one is taken from David Remnick's article, "Joseph Brodsky's Art of Darkness," *The Washington Post*, October 23, 1987.

6   Loseff, Стихотворения и поэмы, 576.

George L. Kline

TABLE 1

'DESTRUCTIVE' TRIPLE DACTYLIC RHYMES IN BRODSKY'S '1972'

Rhyme position: → First	Second	Third
Level: → spiritual/moral	psychological/emotional	physical/biological

Stanza

1. (a) fortochku='ventilation pane in a storm window)

   koftochku='blouse' (which a young woman refuses to remove

   kostochku='(cherry) pit (on which I slip)

   (b) that through which the bird (muse) no longer enters , i.e., failure of poetic creativity

   loss of sexual attractiveness

   exhaustion of physical and biological energy

2. (a) starenie='growing old'

   struenie=(sluggish) flow (of the blood)

   stroenie='shape': the (once handsome) shape (of [my] legs [now] hurts my eyes)

   (b) moving toward silence and nothingness

   cooling of the passions

   physical ugliness that comes with age

3. (a) raskaialos'=(the body) 'has repented' (of its passions)

   bared skalilos'=(the body) 'has showed its teeth', i.e., has laughed

   karies='caries', 'tooth decay'

   (b) I have repented (as I face approaching death)

   my emotional responses (laughing, crying) were in vain

   disintegration of the body

8. (a) trusosti='timidity', 'cowardice'

   trudnosti='difficulty' (of carrying out the act)

   trupnosti='corpseness', 'corpselike condition'

   (b) moral weakness or inertia (which keeps one from committing suicide)

   psychological difficulty of self-destruction

   (future) biological deadness, which is reflected in present moral weakness and psychological inertia

13. (a) otchaian'ia='despair'

   odichaniia='going wild', 'going to seed'

   molchaniia='silence'

   (b) this poem is not a howl of despair

   . . .but the result of (my) going wild

   . . .and the first shriek of (my) silence, i.e., the onset of my dying, lapsing into non-speaking

KEY (a) Transliterated Russian word and literal meaning;

(b) symbolic or metaphorical meaning in the given context

George Kline's mapping of "'destructive' triple dactylic rhymes" in Brodsky's poem "1972" *polysyllabic nouns, verbs, adjectives and participles conjugate (that is, change their endings) in accordance with six cases and three genders. English, with its rigid order, shorter words and precious little change in word endings, is hardly a happy counterpart. 'There is nothing odder,' Brodsky admitted, 'than to apply an analytical device to a synthetic phenomenon; for instance, to write in English about a Russian poet.'*[7]

Is it possible that he didn't really understand that English doesn't have that kind of elasticity? Valentina Polukhina once told me that his motto was, "Nothing is impossible." Well, some things are.

Serious Russian poetry uses dactylic rhymes—Nekrasov, Akhmatova, Pasternak, all used them. But it's obvious that the danger with dactylic rhymes in serious English poetry is that it's very easy to slide over into Ogden Nash and "Timbuktu." You don't want something funny in a serious poem. I don't think there is anything funny about the Russian "1972," but very often the English is bordering on funny or awkward or clunky.

But the gentle irony is hinted at, even in the translation.

I don't know what to do with that poem. It's a wonderful poem, somebody ought to do something. There is no point, it seems to me, in that case, trying to reproduce the form. Maybe do a plain prose version with lots of commentary.

In this poem, as you have noted, there is that semantic slide—a downward one—from "higher" meanings to "lower" ones. So to "rattle" something, that something has to be strong in the first place. In English, rhymes are "rattled" already—especially to a Russian ear.

You have mapped out the "slide" in several stanzas. Let's go back to the first:

> *Птица уже не влетает в форточку.*
> *Девица, как зверь, защищает кофточку.*
> *Подскользнувшись о вишневую косточку, . . .*

> *A bird no longer flies into my open window.*
> *A maiden, with a beast's ferocity, defends the buttons on her shirt.*
> *Having slipped on a cherry pit. . . .*

---

7   Leon Aron, "A World Fiercely Oberved," *Wall Street Journal,* January 15, 2011.

From the cultural/moral of the bird, or perhaps muse, no longer enters—that is the failure of poetic creativity, to the second, psychological/emotional level, the loss of sexual attractiveness. Then the final "slide" to slipping and falling on a cherry pit—the exhaustion of physical and biological energy.

And back to that thirteenth stanza.

The first line on the cultural/moral level—this is not a howl of despair. Then the slide to the psychological/emotional level, "going to seed," as it were. And the final lapse into silence, non-speaking. That is, the onset of dying, lapsing into the state of non-speaking.

A theme that has haunted him since "Nunc Dimittis," or, as you pointed out earlier, even before, in "Gorbunov and Gorchakov": "Life is but talk hurled in the face of silence."

Yes. This poem, written in November and December of 1972, echoes that same parallel between life and speech, and death and silence. It has that urgent sense of the impending end, of irrecoverable loss.

And, for the poet, the final extinction in silence.

The silence of eternity. In this poem he declares: "to grow old is to lose the use of the organ / of hearing, an organ directed toward silence." In other words, the increasing deafness of the old is a preparation for the silence of death.

Since the advent of free verse, and its inevitable deterioration, do you think that English speakers have lost their flexibility for listening to meter and rhyme? I mean, these verse forms are used in the poetry of many languages, not just Russian. The reaction for English-language listeners says more about us than the verse form itself.

The same with rhymes. To many of us today, perfect rhymes sound like Hallmark cards. But I think that problem is not necessarily the exhaustion of rhymes. We've lost our taste for them. It's not the fault of the rhymes but the fault of our ears.

Well, you may be right. You were quoting from Weissbort yesterday. I think there is certain truth to that. Joseph was trying to . . . how did he put it?

He argued that Brodsky "was trying to Russianize English, not respecting the genius of the English language, . . . he wanted the transfer between the languages to take place without drastic changes, this being achievable only if English itself was changed."

I do think there is some truth to that. I was thinking of the poem, remember the poem that Seamus Heaney wrote? I remember something about an automobile. Do you remember that?

The poem was called "Audenesque," in memory of Joseph Brodsky, and begins:

> *Joseph, yes, you know the beat.*
> *Wystan Auden's metric feet*
> *Marched to it, unstressed and stressed,*
> *Laying William Yeats to rest.*

It continues:

> *Politically incorrect*
> *Jokes involving sex and sect,*
> *Everything against the grain.*
> *Drinking, smoking like a train.*

It was very large and very strong and really, in a way, very gently critical, one might say, as well as very well loving and reverent. There was something in it about how Brodsky was like a race car driver and the race car was English and Joseph was driving it with his foot pressed to the floor.

Yes. Here.

> *Nose in air, foot to the floor,*
> *Revving English like a car*
> *You hijacked when you robbed its bank*
> *(Russian was your reserve tank).*

Worshipped language can't undo
Damage time has done to you:
Even your peremptory trust
In words alone here bites the dust.[8]

"Lullaby of Cape Cod"

Let's discuss the history behind a poem you half-translated in 1977. As we all know, Anthony Hecht made a controversial translation, that nevertheless remains the definitive one to date. I was rather startled at what Gifford said about "Lullaby of Cape Cod."[9] I'll quote it in full, after he warns about the perils of "creeping verbosity":

> *Anthony Hecht is a gifted manipulator of words, and all would be well with his spirited version of "Lullaby of Cape Cod," if it did not suggest, say, a more expansive Louis MacNeice rather than Brodsky. His ingenuity is beyond question, but he has been too indulgent, actually in some stanzas exceeding the number of lines by half as many again. Where Brodsky writes of the looking-glass effect of exchanging one empire for another that "your parting . . . has been displaced to the left," this becomes:*
>
> > *the mirror's revelation that the part in your hair*
> > *that you meticulously placed on the left side*
> > *mysteriously shows up on the right.*
>
> *"The thought of Nothingness" has to be "a queer, vertiginous thought" and "tails" (of a coin) "its opposite (tails), its double, its underside." "Death" is glossed as "that punctuation mark," "the clockface" as "a broad, bottomless sea." Thus an important poem loses its admirable tautness. The reader's mind is given no work to do, because Hecht has removed the need for what Mandelstam always expected from his audience, the power of divination; and most readers of poetry are lazy enough anyway in an age dominated by prose.*

At the last moment, Joseph turned to you for a translation to publish.

---

8   Seamus Heaney, "Audenesque," in *Electric Light* (New York: Farrar, Straus and Giroux, 2001), 77-80.

9   Henry Gifford, "Idioms in Interfusion," *Times Literary Supplement*, October 17, 1980, 148.

Joseph phoned and said we've only got maybe two and a half weeks, but could you finish your translation? He said Hecht's translation has some gorgeous English in it, but it's ninety-six lines longer than the original. Well, it wasn't quite that many, I counted it, but it was a lot longer by several dozen lines. And Gifford brings that out in his *TLS* review. It's inexcusable.

You are both very different translators, with very different approaches to translation and strengths. So what did you say to this unusual request?

Of course, I emphasized that I couldn't complete my version in such a short time. It took me several hundred hours to complete the fourteen stanzas of "The Butterfly." Overall, "Lullaby" is twice as long. So Hecht's version, inflated as it was, appeared in *A Part of Speech* in 1980.

Hecht was a poet and he could write lovely lines. But I don't know—did I ever tell you about my correspondence with him?

I don't actually want to but I'll tell you briefly. It's up at Yale, you can find it. Well let's see, I was in England. I can't tell you exactly what year this was.

May and June, 1977. I have it here, from Emory University, where Hecht's papers are.

I'd met Hecht at least briefly once. I don't know if I had corresponded with him before, but I had his address and I sent him a *New York Times* review that included a warm and generous paragraph on Joseph, with a short note. And I may have said something about translation of the "Cape Cod Lullaby."

You did. You mentioned that John Russell's New York Times *review on "The Arts in the Seventies" noted that you were translating "Cape Cod Lullaby," which, you wrote, "may have come as a surprise." Incidentally, you also noted that you were working on this particular translation in "Working with Brodsky," in the spring and autumn 1977 issue of* Paintbrush. *So, hardly a secret.*

You continued in your letter: "Joseph tells me that you've agreed to do it, working with an interlineal version. I would be delighted to defer to you, but in this particular case the poem is very close to me, and I've already invested a great deal of time and energy. . . . If you haven't yet gone too far, would you be willing to do something else for the Farrar, Straus & Giroux volume? Much of importance is still unclaimed." You modestly added that you hoped every poem you translated would be "redone by a real poet."

He came back with a very nasty short note, not thanking me at all or even acknowledging that I'd sent him the review.

I have it here. He is "surprised and shocked" at your "proprietary feeling" and "vested interest." He says Brodsky himself invited him to tackle this particular poem. He says your letter is "out of place," but tosses the poem to you, advising you to tell the poet yourself, and say that you have requested his withdrawal.

> *And after his May 28 note, he wrote again on June 4, still angry, and saying the same thing.*

I assume he had forgotten that he had already written on May 28.

He is again astonished by your "proprietary feeling" and said he will defer and send Joseph your "extraordinary letter."

I thought that if, by a stroke of luck, both he and I produce versions which satisfy both Joseph and Nancy Meiselas of Farrar, Straus & Giroux, then perhaps *both* can be included in *A Part of Speech.* This sort of thing was done, quite successfully I think, in the Montale *Selected Poems* of 1965.

In your June 7 letter, you write that it was never your intention to assert what he had called a "fierce claim" to the poem, and that his language was "quite uncalled for." You generously urged him to forget your letter and continue his translation. Which he did.

> *Hecht didn't get it finished in a hurry. On December 28, 1977, he wrote a letter to Nancy Meiselas that he had sent on his draft of the translated poem. He writes that he is afraid he will disappoint Joseph by forgoing any attempt to render the rhyme and metrical pattern, and so serve "the masterful technical pleasures of the original." He worked with two interlinear texts! Two transcribers of his English texts were confused by the poem, and "neither of them had even a smattering of elementary physics or geometry . . . neither knew who Lobachevsky is, etc." So he wandered in the darkness for awhile, too. He decided, "modestly," he said to work the poem into six-line stanzas of blank verse, "taking occasional liberties here and there." He added that the liberties had not been confined to meter, since he had been working with two interlinear texts which gave him some latitude in interpretation.*

> *However, it's clear that Hecht loved the poem as much as you did. He praised the poem: "its richness of braided themes, its suppleness and variety of*

metaphors, its huge scope, its diversity and homogeneity of matter, all seemed to me at once so dense and so necessary that I felt throughout that any attempt of mine to mimic the poem's formal features would mean a ruthless sacrifice of many of the most splendidly imaginative features of the poem that make it the astonishing achievement that it is."

He wrote: "Let me add immediately that I think the poem is stunning: not simply as fine as anything of Joseph's that I know, but as fine as almost anything in all modern poetry that I can think of. It is deeply moving, full of tenderness, humor, intelligence, and a wild, drunken freedom that is half sadness and half comic."

I never heard from Tony. That brings us back to the phone call. Between that letter and the publication of the translation, Joseph called me. He knew I had started a translation of my own. I don't remember how far I'd gotten. I did do quite a lot of it. Perhaps half, or three-fifths—maybe two fifths, something like that. It's a long, difficult poem. Well everything was difficult, I mean challenging. You had to work very seriously, very hard for quite a while to get it right.

Joseph asked if I could finish it in two-and-a-half weeks. I said that was totally impossible. "What about Tony?" I asked. "What would he say if you didn't publish his translation?" He said, "Oh, well, he can put it in a volume of his own poetry." Maybe he could have, but I'm sure he would've been furious. That was an unpleasant episode.

I wish you had finished yours. I think we would benefit from having both translations to consider—we need more translations of his work generally. The episode was all the more unfortunate considering you had already published "The Butterfly," which I think brought you more clearly into focus as a very important translator of Brodsky.

"The Butterfly"

In 1921, while at Cambridge, Nabokov wrote "Babochka (Vanessa antiopa),"translated by Gavriel Shapiro and Dmitri Nabokov as "Butterfly (Vanessa antiopa)" which concludes:

Yes, I'll recognize you in a Seraph, at the wondrous meeting,
I'll recognize your wings, their sacrosanct design.[10]

Joseph Brodsky wrote his reply with 1973's "The Butterfly." Obviously, this is a case of one poet speaking to another. It was a masterpiece for Brodsky—but also for you. Many consider "The Butterfly" the culmination of your career in translation.

Well, you know every once in a while, I get some wonderful comment from somebody, a bit of gratifying news about my translations. It happened just a couple of months ago, in fact. I have never met or even talked to her on the phone, but a visiting professor from Russia, a fine scholar and a fine person then at a college in Minnesota, related what she said. In an email, a colleague Randall Poole wrote: "Karen Rozenplanz was telling me in raptures about a beautiful profound translation she had read of Brodsky's 'The Butterfly'. It was yours and it is indeed beautiful."

When Joseph Brodsky was asked, in 1979, which of his poems were his favorites, "The Butterfly" was one of two poems he mentioned. (The other was "Letters from the Ming Dynasty.")

In Joseph Brodsky: Conversations, *he told the story of how the poem came to him. He said, "I was trying to combine two things, Beckett and Mozart. Many years ago, in Russia, I was after a girl." By the way, I've been told by those who know that the "girl" was Marina Basmanova, the mother of his son and the dedicatee of so many of his poems. "We left a concert, a Mozart concert, and she told me as we walked down the streets, 'Joseph, everything is lovely about your poetry,' et cetera. 'Well, you know that,' et cetera, 'except you never execute in a poem that lightness and yet gravity which Mozart has.' And that kind of got me. I remembered that very well, and I decided to write that butterfly poem." He added, "Well, I hope I managed. Actually, George Kline did an excellent job translating the poem."*[11]

I remember a few things he said about this poem and Mozart. Some of them are in writing and some of them are now at Yale, but of course I have copies. I probably told you this, he wrote two or three pages of detailed comments

---

10   Vladimir Vladimirovich Nabokov, *Nabokov's Butterflies: Unpublished and Uncollected Writings*, ed. Robert Michael Pyle and Brian Boyd, trans. Dmitri Nabokov (Boston: Beacon, 2000), 103–4.

11   Haven, *Joseph Brodsky: Conversations*, 60.

on my draft of "The Butterfly." The comment relevant to this subject: "Just think of Mozart and Beckett." Later in that same letter, he wrote, "You don't have to include Beckett. The absurd is already there in Mozart." In other words, he was saying Mozart was rich enough and strong enough to include that so you didn't have to appeal to Beckett. He was thinking about the classical structure. Mozart: that's of course the very shape, the butterfly shape, of the stanzas and sort of the absurdity.

I remember somewhere, maybe in an interview, he said, "Well you wanted to know about structure. Do you want to know about organizing a poem? Study Mozart." Yes, he entirely agreed with you. He did love finished structures, I think you could say that, in both music and in architecture.

Henry Gifford wrote in The Times Literary Supplement *of October 17, 1980, that it was "an accomplished rendering of an intricate poem," noting how "identical form can be used felicitously when the translator responds to a poem's movement within its fixities." He cited this stanza:*

> *Should I say that, somehow*
> *you lack all being?*
> *What, then, are my hands feeling*
> *that's so like you?*
> *Such colors can't be drawn*
> *from nonexistence.*
> *Tell me, at whose insistence*
> *Were yours laid on?*
> *Since I'm a mumbling heap*
> *of words, not pigments,*
> *how could your hues be figments*
> *of my conceit?*

Joseph didn't make many changes to this translation . . . did he?

Once, when I had let an overly "Romantic" line or two slip into an early draft of my translation of "Babochka," Joseph said, in effect, "We don't need that. There's enough romanticism in the form of the poem"—that is, with every short line centered on the page.

The reason I've spoken so much about the versions of my translations published in journals before they were published in books is because, as you might have guessed, in almost every case significant revisions occurred in between, mostly prompted by Joseph.

"The Butterfly" is the one exception I can recall. The 1976 *New Yorker* version was the same as the one that appeared in *A Part of Speech*.

I will send you if you haven't seen it. You remember what the British critic Henry Gifford wrote in the 1980 *Times Literary Supplement*? He's the one who said that Brodsky and I were Brodsky's best translators, in his review of *A Part of Speech*. Zak sent it to me as an attachment, but the problem is in the attachment the two stanzas of my translation of "The Butterfly," which were cited, are blocked up against the left-hand side of the page, and it doesn't look right. It looks totally wrong.

It's amazing how that simple typographical move ruins the "Mozartian" delicacy and transparency of the poem. Or to put it the other way around: it's amazing how his device of centering all these short lines brings out the Mozartian delicacy and transparency of the poem.

And that same thing happened, by the way, when the Nobel was announced, and the *New York Times* had a front-page story. I don't remember whether it was on that page or the continuation inside, they quoted a couple of stanzas from "The Butterfly." And again, all up against the left side.

I think David Bethea speaks to this question to some extent. I haven't seen him for quite a while but I used to know him moderately well. In one of his chapters, he quotes practically the entire text of "The Butterfly." Did you notice that? I've got it on my shelf.

Yes. He called it "arguably one of Brodsky's greatest metaphysical creations . . . a verbal butterfly capable of competing with the flight of Mozart's musical notes."

He quotes a stanza or two in Russian and then the same stanza or two in my translation. It's very nice. He has excellent, I think, perceptive comments about the text and also about the translation.

Bethea also points out that Brodsky had "topped" Nabokov with this poem— not that Nabokov provided any real competition as a poet. Joseph's poem has far more "precision": "Brodsky's description is of a different order than that of Nabokov's. It has to do with inherent poetic qualities, with the elaborate stanza form and metrical scheme, themselves as delicate and carefully wrought as the butterfly wing they mimic."[12]

---

12   Bethea, *Joseph Brodsky and the Creation of Exile*, 241–42.

Any more thoughts about the Gifford review?

Just this one. Gifford says Joseph Brodsky is "perhaps the only Russian poet to have known the English Metaphysicals." My goodness, that's a huge thing to say. Is it true?

I think so. I can't think of any other Russian poet who has translated them or talked about them or been influenced by them.

Other poets read English, surely. Of course, John Donne only became well established in the English canon in the 1920s. People forget that he was not widely read in the eighteenth or nineteenth centuries.

Right, that's true. That's part of the reason probably.

But Donne's not the only one. There's Andrew Marvell, Fulke Greville, George Herbert, there's lots of others.

Even Christopher Marlowe. Well, it's a good question. I don't know how to answer it really. I'll think about it.

David Bethea made a more tempered claim. He said, "Brodsky can be called the first and only Russian poet to have mastered the English metaphysical tradition, with its passion for paradox, its 'difficult joining' of the conceit, and its predilection for expressing the large and abstract (beauty, morality) through the small (butterfly)." That claim seems to me more sustainable.

His chapter, "Exile as Pupation: Genre and Bilingualism in the Works of Nabokov and Brodsky," discusses Nabokov's poetry.

It confirms what I was saying about Nabokov as a poet. I don't know that I need to repeat, but he's very intellectual and sort of—how shall I put it?—"artificialist." It doesn't seem to be any spontaneity anywhere and there's very little passion. It's cold. It really is.

And yet Brodsky calls out to Nabokov in the poem.

You mean this:

не высказать ясней,
что в самом деле
мир создан был без цели,
а если с ней,
то цель—не мы.
Друг—энтомолог,
для света нет иголок
и нет для тьмы.

The sixth line is literally, "Friend, entomologist." He is referring to Nabokov, but I had to leave it out. I couldn't figure out any way to get it in.

That's in the remarkable twelfth stanza, which you rendered so beautifully. Here's the whole passage, rendered more literally and without your artistry, in an online version I found that has since disappeared. (And it is flush left, which I know distresses you):

To make it clearer: in fact,
the world was created without an aim,
and if there was an aim,
It's not us.
Friend-entomologist,
There is no needle for light,
nor any for for darkness.

Another translator translated it this way—and centered the lines! In a translation from Judith Pulman in the spring 2013 edition of Ezra:

Friend, entomologist—
in the haystack that's well-
lit you can't find the needle,
nor can you in the darkness.

It's complex, and doesn't translate well, so I find your rendering free, but exceptionally lovely:

Such beauty, set beside
so brief a season,
suggests to our stunned reason

the bleak surmise:
the world was made to hold
no end or telos,
and if—as some would tell us—
there is a goal,
it's not ourselves.
No butterfly collector
can trap light or detect where
the darkness dwells.

To spare your modesty, let's return to that difficult relationship with Nabokov, whose prose had entranced Brodsky in Leningrad.

You probably heard what the Proffers had to report, didn't you?

When the Proffers visited the Nabokovs in Lugano, in 1969, the Nabokovs gave them money to buy presents for Joseph and Nadezhda Mandelstam. Joseph got jeans. He must have been over the moon. Ellendea says that Nabokov was a favorite at that time among the intelligentsia, so a gift from him must have been an important mark of favor.

The Proffers were on very friendly terms with both Nabokov and Brodsky, and it left them in kind of a tough situation sometimes. Nabokov made some very nasty comments about his poetry.

The poem was the long Gorbunov and Gorchakov, *which they had sent to Lugano after they returned home that fall. In a letter to the Proffers, he wrote: "It contains many attractive metaphors and eloquent rhymes . . . but is flawed by incorrectly accented words, lack of verbal discipline, and an overabundance of words in general." Like the emperor's criticism of Mozart: "Too many notes."*

Nabokov concludes: "However, esthetic criticism would be unfair in view of the ghastly surroundings and sufferings implied in every line of the poem."

I forget all that he said but he didn't really have much good to say about the poem. Carl told me all this. He was sort of taken aback and distressed and so on by Nabokov's reaction.

And Carl told Joseph everything, at his insistence, and the poet never forgot or forgave Nabokov.

Maybe this is an interesting point. Do you suppose Carl could have told Joseph about that before Joseph wrote "The Butterfly"? That would be something, wouldn't it?

It certainly would be. The Proffers were back in Russia for New Year's Eve, 1970.

But he could be fixed in his enmities. This from Ellendea Proffer: "Nabokov and Brodsky were both witty people who were sensitive about their literary honor. They were opinionated, ambitious, and intensely competitive. They also shared a hostility to what they understood to be Freudian views of the subconscious."[13] Joseph was pre-Freudian. The Soviet Union bypassed all this self analysis.

Well, the Russians had a little brush with it in the twenties when they translated some Freud and so on.

I know, but it didn't perturb the psychology.

And it was suppressed very soon.

Brodsky didn't have a great self-awareness about his own contradictions.

Well now wait. How about "Odysseus to Telemachus"? Remember the end of it?

Yes. With dreams that are blameless.

I am trying to think how it goes in Russian—". . . i sny tvoi, moi Telemakh, bezgreshny." In your dreams, my Telemachus, well it's literally "sinless." I might have said "blameless." He knew something about the Freudian, Oedipus complex.

---

13 Ellendea Proffer Teasley, *Brodsky among Us: A Memoir* (Boston: Academic Studies Press, 2017), 16. I had read an earlier draft of the memoir.

Well, yes, the theory. But when he stood up at the Michigan stadium years later and he said you could measure a man by how well he treats women, he didn't seem to have an awareness of how he himself treated women.

I agree.

Perhaps there was some envy there. That Nabokov was the real polish he aimed towards.

And Nabokov was nowhere near the poet that Joseph was. You agree with that?

I doubt that any Russian poet of the last decades could top Joseph's corpus, but I don't know Nabokov's poetry at all, really. But the point is that . . .

It's sort of academic. It's not exciting. It's not powerful. It doesn't seem original to me. It's formal and correct and all that. His prose, I loved one of his prose works. What's it called? *Pnin.* Have you read that?

I haven't read it for years and I shouldn't talk about it but, to me, he obviously loves this guy, Professor Pnin—unlike his characters in *Lolita*!—and it's very funny in places. He's a professor who is all trained and going to give a lecture on the humanism of Pushkin somewhere, at Sarah Lawrence or Mount Holyoke, and misses his stop.

It's just all full of crazy things like that. He's an absent-minded professor and when he speaks English he says, "The *quittance*, I must have the *quittance*" when he means "the receipt." *Kvitantsiia* is the Russian word for "receipt." But nobody understands him.

He's a lovable character. He's fumbling and awkward and really lovable. It's a great book. I can't say I don't warm to Nabokov. I warm at least to that. Look, Brodsky said, "*Dar* is a great work of Russian fiction." That's *The Gift* in English.

I think he said that also about the other one, *Dar,* and *An Invitation to a Beheading.* Those were earlier. Those were early, from the 1930s, and Joseph loved them and admired them.

Joseph had such a conflicted relationship with the legacy of Nabokov—another Russian writer who turned his hand to writing in English. Critics inevitably compared them—not always favorably to Brodsky.

One thing that such critics forget is how enormously difficult it was for Brodsky, who didn't know a word of English until he was in his teens, to write poems directly in English or to translate his own Russian poetry into English.

On a much smaller scale, I experienced something like this challenge myself. Stephen Spender, as the consultant to poetry, invited Brodsky to the 1974 Spoleto festival in Italy. But the Soviets, through their embassy in Rome, applied blackmail. They had threatened to withdraw permission for a provincial Soviet dance company to perform if "that non-poet Brodsky was permitted to appear." So Spender, a friend of Brodsky's, gave way and "disinvited" the poet. Brodsky, who was already in London, took it in good grace, saying that he could appear at Spoleto later but that this was the only opportunity for the "little dancers from Perm." Spender wouldn't even let me play Brodsky tapes, for fear of offending the Soviets, except in a very small group in someone's room.

On that occasion, a young British poet had written a poem of welcome and appreciation for those dancers, and asked me to translate it into Russian. I explained to him that I translated only from Russian to English, my native language. But he persisted. So, with great reluctance, I finally sat down to translate his poem into Russian. It was very hard work and I wasn't satisfied with the result, but I let him present it to the visiting dancers. What they made of it, I don't know. But I heard later that the poet had let a native speaker of Russian read my translation, and that the Russian had simply laughed. At that point I had been reading, writing, and speaking Russian for nearly twenty-five years. I had read and appreciated the poetry of Pushkin, Blok, Akhmatova, Pasternak, and Tsvetaeva. But translating an English poem into adequate literary Russian was beyond my powers.

So I felt a great deal of sympathy for Brodsky. I also considered it quite unfair to compare him, as certain critics did, unfavorably, to Nabokov, whose well-off family provided him with English governesses and tutors from his preschool years.

Yet Joseph got so far without tutors.

It's hard for me to believe, but he really taught himself to read Polish. He read Faulkner in Polish. He read Kafka in Polish. It's astonishing.

And of course he was reading Zbigniew Herbert and Czesław Miłosz. Miłosz reached out to him almost as soon as he was expelled from his rodina in 1972.

By the time of the Selected, *he was already translating Miłosz, and calling him one of the major poets of the twentieth century—eight years before the Polish poet's Nobel. At that time, very few in the West had even heard of him.*

I was reading a couple of reviews to send to you. One is a brief review, but it made a very interesting point. It said, and this is a review of course of *Selected Poems,* "These poems display a consciousness that can be called nothing other than religious." That's what Miłosz said, that Brodsky was a pious man in a sense of having a very strong sense of the sacredness of being.

You quote that at the end of your essay about "Presepio," and it's from my interview with him. What Czesław Miłosz said to me: "Brodsky was very sensitive to the sacredness of being. Yes. That's why I call him pious. I didn't ask him if he believes in God—you felt in him that openness to the sacred."[14]

You could put it that way. The sacredness of human existence. The sacredness of language, and so on.

I like what William Logan wrote in his review of the Nativity Poems, *back in 2001: "Brodsky, who liked to pass Christmas in Venice, that sinking monument to the decay of architecture and belief, saw with what magnificence a skeptic could contemplate centuries past—these poems express a fealty to the past without being enslaved by it. And there is, almost like frailty, the doubt beneath Brodsky's doubt—you sense he felt the myths might just possibly be true."[15]*

---

14 Cynthia L. Haven, ed., *Czesław Miłosz: Conversations* (Jackson: University Press of Mississippi, 2006), 197.
15 Logan, "All Over the Map," 78.

Brodsky's friends celebrate Stockholm's 1987 Nobel award. Standing, from left to right: Masha Vorobiova, Roger Straus, Margo Picken, Maria Modig, Kees Verheul, two unidentified women, Roberto Calasso, Véronique Schiltz, Fleur Calasso, Joseph Brodsky, George Kline, Natalia Gorbanevskaia, Lev Loseff, Jonas Modig, Jelena Jangfeldt-Jakubovitch, unidentified woman. On their knees, from left to right: Hans Ohlson, Bengt Jangfeldt, Giovanni Buttafava. (Photo from Bengt Jangfeldt archives)

Chapter 8

"What did you do in World War II?"

In Ludmila Shtern's Brodsky: A Personal Memoir,[1] *there's a photo of Joseph wearing the military cap of his "friend and translator." That's you. Can you tell me how your officer's cap wound up on Joseph Brodsky's head in New York City?*

It was my World War II service cap. That photo of Joseph wearing the cap and Maria saluting was taken by M. Petrov at one of Joseph's legendary birthday parties—actually, the last one, on May 24, 1995. That party was at his home, 22 Pierrepont Street in Brooklyn Heights, where he had lived for three years, after leaving his long-time residence, 44 Morton Street in Greenwich Village, in March 1993.

The birthday parties, although always in his home, were always—so far as I can remember—lavishly catered by Roman Kaplan of the famous "Russkii samovar" in midtown Manhattan, with several members of his Russian-speaking, mostly young and masculine staff.

What did you usually do for his birthday?

Well, I always brought or sent him something. A couple of times, when I was out of the country, or he was, we exchanged phone calls. But the birthday presents I took to the party, or put in the mail, ranged from the severely practical, a pair of tires because his were badly worn out and I feared for his

---

1   Ludmila Shtern, *Brodsky: A Personal Memoir* (Fort Worth: Baskerville, 2004).

Joseph Brodsky was fascinated by George Kline's war experience, and they took turns wearing his wartime navigator's service cap at Brodsky's last birthday party on May 24, 1995. (Photo courtesy the Kline Family Estate)

safety behind the wheel. On his fortieth birthday in 1980 I gave him a set of late Mozart quartets on two LP vinyl records. Another time I gave him an album of Purcell operas including *Dido and Aeneas*. On his fiftieth birthday I wrote him a poem. Perhaps I'll be able to find it. As I recall, it had end rhymes in Russian and Italian, as well as English.[2]

At different times, I'd given him various things connected with service as a navigator, flying out of Southern Italy during World War II. I remember giving him a pair of the small wings—not the big official wings that I wore as a celestial navigator, but little ones that were shaped like a propeller.

---

2   The poem "To Joseph on Turning Fifty" is included at the end of this volume.

A wartime wedding: George Kline married Virginia Harrington "Ginny" Hardy in a simple civil ceremony where he is stationed in Texas, on April 17, 1943. (Photo used courtesy the Kline Family Estate)

For Joseph, everything naval or military had an allure. His father had been a war photographer and wore a uniform—he was proud of that. As a child, he had a preoccupation with the heroic *and the* manly. *His boyhood dream was to be a naval officer. But as a Jew, he wasn't eligible.*

I once gave him a photograph—you know how he loved photographs of his friends. He had them all over his study wall, both in Leningrad and Greenwich Village. I remember seeing a photo on his wall at 44 Morton Street of his old and close friend Tomas Venclova at the Vatican with Pope John Paul XXIII. The photograph I gave Joseph was about 8" by 10"; it showed the commander of the Army Air Corps base in Pueblo, Colorado, a handsome friendly colonel, pinning the Distinguished Flying Cross on my uniform. That wasn't when I was flying combat missions—a total of fifty of them between February and July 1944—I mean, I *earned* the DFC in combat, but I received it in the fall of 1944, when I was serving as a navigation instructor. It's a nice picture of me as a young officer. I was then a first lieutenant. The base commander is shaking my hand, pinning the DFC on my uniform. As I recall, Joseph had that on his study wall for quite a while.

Back to the photo in Ludmila Shtern's memoir. The editor of that book sent me the proof sheets, which I read carefully, correcting a few errors and even more omissions. For me the most striking omission was the caption of this photograph, which in the proofs simply announced that "somebody had given him this cap and he loved to wear it." After I sent in my correction, this was changed to "Friend and translator George Kline had given him his World War II navigator's service cap, and he loved to wear it." Arriving in Brooklyn Heights for what turned out to be Joseph's last birthday, I thought that this would be a rather special gift. Actually, I didn't at this point intend it as a permanent gift. Rather I was planning to lend it to him for a few months. Anyway, I took the cap with me to the party, and he really glowed when I handed it to him. He said well, I just love this cap. He said it several times. He said, "I feel as though I was a part of World War II." And in some sense, of course, he was.

There were lots of pictures of Joseph wearing my cap on that occasion, not just the one that Ludmila Shtern published. I've seen half a dozen other pictures where he was with various people. I have one of Joseph alone, wearing the cap, in a cobalt blue shirt and blue jeans. There is another of the two of us. In one Joseph is wearing the cap, and I have my arm around his shoulders. In a third I'm wearing the cap. It was pure luck that it fitted Joseph perfectly. In fact, in the pictures of the two of us, he is wearing it better, at a more appropriate angle, than I am. I pushed the cap too far back from my forehead.

He was, forever, a child of that war, wasn't he?

Well, here's what he actually said. I think it was at the birthday party, it was either when I first gave him or offered him the cap or maybe when I was leaving, he said, "Well, I always thought of myself as part of that war." I remember that phrase.

I remember something else about that party. Joseph even spoke about wearing it as he was "going into the box." Well he meant dying and being in a coffin, basically. That was his slightly poetic, or at least unusual, way of putting that. He didn't say it in a dismal or gloomy way, he was quite cheerful when he was saying it.

And I remember saying to Barry Rubin, Joseph's friend, who had translated several of his poems as well as his Nobel lecture, and was with Baryshnikov, Gennady Shmakov, and me at Joseph's first honorary degree at Yale in 1978. Barry was at the party with his bride, I told you something about that. They'd been married, I guess, a year or two. Anyway, I just said something like, "You know, he's always talking about going into the box—I wish he wouldn't." I don't remember exactly what Barry Rubin said, but it was something like, "Well, that's just Joseph's way of talking."

Well, but it wasn't just talk—not at the end. He was only fifty-five when he died, in the early hours of 28 January 1996.

I attended the funeral, which was in a Episcopalian church in Brooklyn.[3] Well, I've talked quite a bit about that, you have the little paper on his

---

3   A viewing took place at Greenwich Village Funeral Home on Bleecker Street shortly after the death, to allow close friends to say farewell to the poet. Kline is describing the funeral that was held on 1 February 1996, at Grace Episcopal Church in Brooklyn Heights, near Brodsky's home. It was followed by a larger memorial service for the public at St. John the Divine Episcopal Church, in Manhattan, on March 8. On June 21, 1997, there was a burial at San Michele Cemetery in his beloved Venice. At that time, his grave was marked by a modest wooden cross. Since Brodsky was baptized neither in the Orthodox or the Catholic Church, he was buried in the Protestant area of the cemetery, perhaps fitting for the man who once said, "I regard myself as a Calvinist: that is, one who fears severe judgment of one's own views, one's own endeavors" (Haven, *Joseph Brodsky: Conversations*, 179).
         However, rumors persist of a secret baptism during the Stalin years. I found a reference to a baptism in the translator Daniel Weissbort's papers, at the London home of Valentina Polukhina, and asked her for details after my 2018 visit. The poet Viktor Krivulin had told her that Natalya Grudinina, who took an active part in defending Brodsky during the trial and after fighting for his release (she died in 1999), became friendly with Brodsky's mother in the years after her son's emigration in 1972. Maria Volpert Brodskaya confided to Grudinina that Joseph's Russian nanny had him baptized in secret without his mother's permission during the evacuation to Cherepovets—"most likely it wasn't done in a church but in somebody's home, maybe in a former priest's place," said Polukhina. Such baptisms were commonplace at the time—even Putin was secretly baptized in 1952. So was Polukhina: "I myself was born in a Siberian village in the family of Polish exiles and was baptized as a child but learned about it only when I had grown up. It simply was too dangerous to mention it to a child who might mention it to his school friends." She added: "I can also remind you one of Joseph Brodsky's pronouncements: 'I am a bad Russian, a bad Jew, and a bad Christian, but a good poet.' Only a Christian can say 'I am a bad Christian.' I cannot say, 'I am a bad Muslim' because I am not a Muslim." Certainly such a baptism would establish an interesting parallel with the secret baptism of another eminent Russian poet, Boris Pasternak, a few decades earlier.

"Presepio," that was called "Joseph Brodsky's *Presepio* in the Context of His Other Nativity Poems."[4] I say quite a lot about it, but I was thinking that he was, as Miłosz said, a pious man in several senses.

You quote my interview with Miłosz in it. He said that Brodsky was "one for whom 'reverence toward being' was essential," and who "was very sensitive to the sacredness of being."[5]

Anyway, at the early part of the service or at the beginning of the service, I guess, a small group of people came in and the only one I recall immediately recognizing was Véronique. I have never seen a human being who looked so devastated. Russians have this expression *zaplakannoe litso*, you know, a face that's been—I don't know how you put it—someone who's been sobbing for a while. She looked beaten up, the face of a woman who has been crying and sobbing, more than anybody there. It was obvious she had been devastated.

I remember Susan Sontag reached out her hand and caressed his coffin as it went by leaving the church. She reached out her hand and touched the coffin and sort of caressed it. I'm sure many people did that. After that, I couldn't see.

You know about all of the Christian symbolism at his funeral? He had a cross on his chest and so on?[6]

Susan Sontag had a few words about that: "I never felt that Joseph was a Jewish author. We never talked about religious matters. I am completely secular, and I also felt that he was completely secular. . . . He was interested in Christianity because of its domination of European culture. I feel the same way. When I saw him laid out in the Catholic funeral home in downtown Manhattan and buried in a Protestant cemetery in Venice[7]—I was at both

---

4   George L. Kline, "Brodsky's Presepio in the Context of His Other Nativity Poems," *A Journal of Russian Thought* 7 (2007): 67-80.

5   Cynthia L. Haven, "'A Sacred Vision': An interview with Czesław Miłosz," in Haven, *Czesław Miłosz: Conversations*, 73.

6   The cross on Brodsky's chest had belonged to Brodsky's Jewish mother, perhaps a gift from one of her friends and, in Soviet Russia, a reminder of gentler, more civilized times. At least one person remembered the cross being pressed into his hands at the Bleecker Street viewing as well as the funeral.

7   The Greenwich Village Funeral home is not "Catholic," but serves all faiths. The San Michele Cemetery in Venice is not specifically Protestant, but has a Protestant section, where Brodsky was buried. Cf. note 3 above.

funerals—I was surprised. People, when they die, are at the mercy of their relatives. . . . This was his material: there was Horace, there was Ovid and there was Auden, there was Akhmatova and Tsvetaeva. Why does Judaism have to come into it? Why does Christianity come into it?"[8]

Curiously, she cites Auden and Akhmatova, who were both instrumental in Joseph's worldview. He had written, "Akhmatova's poetry contains the unique lesson of Christian ethics in literature—a lesson all the more valuable in that it was given at a time and under circumstances in which man was distinguished from the animal rather by the number of his extremities than in any other way."[9] *He told Solomon Volkov: "Akhmatova transformed you into* Homo sapiens *with just the tone of her voice or the turn of her head. . . . In conversation with her, or simply drinking vodka with her, you became a Christian, a human being in the Christian sense of that word, faster than by reading the appropriate texts or attending church."*[10] *He spoke of Auden in much the same terms.*

But we're a long way away from your hat, now. And the party.

Back to the hat. Joseph said, "I'm going to wear it right into the box"—in almost exactly those words, perhaps when I first gave it to him, or sometime between then and when I left—I always had to leave these parties before they were over to catch a train back to Philadelphia.

At the end of the party, Joseph was still wearing the cap and I guess my thought was, "Well, I'll take it now." I made a gesture or said something and he looked, as I recall it, pained as though he thought it was a permanent gift and how could I take it?

That must have been an awkward misunderstanding.

I'm not sure. I may be overinterpreting. I do remember saying this, "Well, Joseph, do you want to keep it?" He said, with great feeling, "Oh, yes, I do!" I was really surprised by how intense he was about it. I said, "Well, look. Let's do it this way. You keep it until we meet again." He was happy with that, it seemed. But, of course, we never met again, although we had

---

8   Polukhina, *Brodsky through the Eyes*, 2:331.

9   Brodsky, "Translating Akhmatova," *New York Review of Books* 20, no. 3 (August 9, 1973): 9-11. Translation by Carl R. Proffer.

10   Solomon Volkov, *Conversations with Joseph Brodsky: A Poet's Journey through the Twentieth Century* (New York: Free Press, 1998) 207.

one long phone conversation in December of that year. He died in January 1996. He kept the cap as long as he lived. Maria told me after his death that he had been wearing it pretty constantly until the week before he died. Actually, despite being more than fifty years old, the cap in 1995 was in pretty decent condition. But when I eventually got it back, I believe it was in 2010, it had deteriorated pretty badly.

How did he come to feel such a kinship with your own war experiences?

Joseph had a very strong interest in World War II. One of the first things he asked me—not in the first hour but probably the first week—when I was with him in Leningrad in '67 was: "What did you do in World War II?" That was the question he asked a lot of people. When I told him he seemed quite excited.

I guess you know that I was the navigator in a heavy bomber crew. I flew out of Italy in 1944 on a total of fifty combat missions.

So you were bombing Germany?

Seldom. We mostly bombed Eastern European oil fields, Ploesti, and various places in Romania and Bulgaria. That was the main source of the German's oil supply, and that was one thing that was effective. Many of our planes were shot down either by flak or German fighters, and some of our bombs missed their targets, but on the whole we reduced the flow of petroleum to German tanks, planes, trucks, jeeps, and so on. By the end of the war, the Germans had many shiny new tanks, trucks, jeeps, and planes that they couldn't drive or fly, because of a lack of fuel. Thank God for that.

I didn't know about that chunk of war history.

Well, there's some dispute about how much effect the bombing had, but I've looked into the question and I'm convinced that the effect was major. Other factors may have been involved, sabotage on the ground and things like that. Of course when we bombed, let's say, a certain oil field, oil storage tank, or the railroad tracks leading to it, the Germans, within a matter of days, repaired most of the damage, so we kept going back. We bombed elsewhere—around Vienna, the submarine pens in southern France, etc. I think only once did we actually bomb a target in Germany, but of course Austria was a part of the greater German Reich, as they said in those days.

Tolia Naiman, of course, was with us when I was talking with Joseph in Leningrad in 1967 or 1968. Certainly he heard about it—if not directly from me, then from Joseph. He writes about that in his book. I guess that it's never been translated. It's called "Slavnyi konets besslavnykh pokolenii."[11] In English, it would be "The glorious end of inglorious generations." Anyway, he writes this on page 220: "In the war he [Kline] was a military flyer, which raised the temperature of our feelings toward him."

A whole generation lived through that war, but why was Joseph, in particular, so intensely interested in this history, and for so long—more than so many of his peers?

Partly, I suppose, because he lived through it as a child. When I was bombing, in the summer of '44, he was four years old and living with his grandparents. His mother served, for a while, as an interpreter in a German POW camp. I guess you knew that.

He knew everything on combat aircraft of the Second World War; when asked on what airline he was flying to Europe he said: Luftwaffe.[12] Some people thought his relationship to the war must have been related to the Holocaust, and the burden of the Holocaust. I don't see it. His experience was centered on his city, Leningrad, and the Siege. Some find hints of the Holocaust in "Isaac and Abraham," but they are that—hints. A few other poems have overt Jewish references as well.

He was obviously a Jew in Russia—as he notes, he couldn't say a Russian "r" (Jews swallowed their "r"s). Antisemitism was on the rise during his childhood, and his father was dismissed from his post as naval officer because he was a Jew. And although he remembers schoolyard bullying for being a Jew and fistfights, too, he emerged defiant:

> I'm a Jew. One hundred percent. You can't be more Jewish than I am. Papa, mama—no question. No mixing, no intermarriage. But that's not the only reason I'm a Jew. I realize I tend to state things in absolute terms. But—if I were to define for myself some notion of Higher Being, I would have to say that

---

11   Anatoly Naiman, *Slavnyi konets besslavnykh pokolenii* (Moscow: Vagrius, 1998).

12   This sally was recently recounted in Adam Zagajewski's tribute "Zagajewski: Gdy pytali Brodskiego, jaką linią leci do Europy, odpowiadał: Luftwaffe," *Gazeta Wyborcza*, 23 May, 2020.

it comes down to pure force. This is the God of the Old Testament. I sense this, I feel this, in the absence of any proof at all."[13]

And he was loyal to Russia, its culture, its heritage, most of all its language. Wasn't the Siege of Leningrad bad enough? His first years were lived under its shadow, and followed with Leningrad's terrible postwar privations.

The blockade lasted more than two years; more than two million people died from hunger, cold, or disease. The Germans were able to prevent almost all resupply of food, fuel, or medicine from getting through to the people of Leningrad. Anybody who was involved or living in Leningrad during the blockade, as he partly was,[14] would be interested.

But in Joseph's case, I think it was more. I think he tended to judge people by what they had done during World War II. He told me about several such cases. One was socially at a very high level. In December 1987, he had dinner at the Nobel ceremonies with the king and queen of Sweden. They placed him beside the queen. He told me later that she was maybe ten or a dozen years older than he was. At this banquet—it was fairly daring of him—he said, "Your Majesty, what were you doing during World War II?" Do you know what the answer was?

No.

He was a little bit suspicious, I think, after he heard the answer. It turned out the queen had spent most of World War II in Argentina. There were some famous German Nazis there.

That's odd. Actually, she was several years younger than he was. Queen Silvia was born during the war, in 1943, in Heidelberg. Her father was German and her mother Brazilian. Her father was a member of the Nazi Party, and the family hunkered down in São Paulo after the war for a decade, but she couldn't be held responsible for where her parents transported her. It's curious that Joseph should have held it against her in any way.

---

13 Brodsky, "Bol'shaia kniga interv'iu," 656—also cited in Loseff, *Joseph Brodsky: A Literary Life*, 24.

14 Actually, in December 1941, Brodsky and his mother were evacuated to Cherepovets, and didn't return to Leningrad until 1944. However, he did experience life under siege: the Brodsky home on Obvodnyi Canal had been bombed and they were moved to 2 Ryleev Street, apartment 10.

I don't know the stories of who, at least after the war, turned up in South America. And I don't really know anything about the queen's politics during the war or later.

But that incident, too, shows how deeply he had internalized the war and everything about it. The war experience affected some more than others— even in the United States. My mother was always reading about World War II and watching TV documentaries. Being Hungarian, she certainly had strong opinions about Yalta.

Where was she during the war? Was she in Hungary then?

No, her family had emigrated. Still, being a young woman at the time of the war in the United States was a pivotal experience for her. It certainly wasn't true of her whole generation.

I think that's right.

So that's my point. Certainly his preoccupation with World War II wasn't matched by others of his peers. Does Naiman talk about the war quite that much or . . . ?

That's a good question.

Yes, of course Joseph survived the Siege of Leningrad, but he was five years old when it was over. It's interesting that it became such a large part of his psychology.
You recalled Joseph saying, "I am part of that war"—was that the phrase you used?

Yes, he said, "I've always felt myself a part of that war." That's the way he put it.
Or perhaps he said he "took part in" the war—maybe he put it that way. In a sense, he did. He suffered through it, his friends and relatives died of starvation, cold, or disease. It wasn't as though he was actually in Argentina or somewhere. Or that the war was only a distant rumor. He once told me his impression of the canned Spam that the Russians received from the United States during the war.

Well, Spam seems to be a generational memory, too. He even wrote an essay about it, I believe.

He loved to have it to eat. It doubtless helped keep him alive during and just after the war. But he was even more impressed by the key opener, something he had never seen before.

The photo in the Shtern book has Maria in it. Joseph's wearing the cap. Maria is saluting. Yes, that's a nice one. Somebody took at least two pictures and I think probably more like four with Brodsky wearing the cap and my not being with him, and then my wearing the cap and he not.

As you said, it was the last of the birthdays. It had been a long journey for both of you together, over twenty-seven years. And through a startlingly successful exile.

You've pointed out that the exiled Czech novelist Josef Skvorecky distinguished between two contrasting approaches to being a writer-in-exile, using Ovid and Joseph Conrad to exemplify them. Where would you place the later Joseph—that is, Joseph Brodsky?

With Conrad. Rather than wasting himself in nostalgia for his lost homeland—like Ovid, in the Crimea—he threw his considerable energy and imagination into the language, literature, and culture of his adopted homeland.

And yet, he always remained a Russian—a European, too.

Like Goethe, Joseph Brodsky, was, and indeed always had been, a "good European."

Joseph Brodsky on California Street, San Francisco, in December 1988. (Photo: Grisha Freidin, originally published on his blog *The Noise of Time*)

Chapter 9

Poems by Joseph Brodsky, Translated by George L. Kline

Elegy for John Donne

John Donne has sunk in sleep . . . All things beside
are sleeping too: walls, bed, and floor—all sleep.
The table, pictures, carpets, hooks and bolts,
clothes-closets, cupboards, candles, curtains—all
now sleep: the washbowl, bottle, tumbler, bread,
breadknife and china, crystal, pots and pans,
bed-sheets and nightlamp, chests of drawers, a clock,
a mirror, stairway, doors. Night everywhere,
night in all things: in corners, in men's eyes,
in bed-sheets, in the papers on a desk,
in the worm-eaten words of sterile speech,
in logs and fire-tongs, in the blackened coals
of a dead fireplace—in each thing.
In undershirts, boots, stockings, shadows, shades
behind the mirror; in the backs of chairs,
in bed and washbowl, in the crucifix,
in linen, in the broom beside the door,
in slippers. All these things have sunk in sleep.
Yes, all things sleep. The window. Snow beyond.
A roof-slope, whiter than a tablecloth,
the roof's high ridge. A neighborhood in snow,

carved to the quick by this sharp windowframe.
Arches and walls and windows—all asleep.
Wood paving-blocks, stone cobbles, gardens, grills.
No light will flare, no turning wheel will creak . . .
Chains, walled enclosures, ornaments, and curbs.
Doors with their rings, knobs, hooks are all asleep—
their locks and bars, their bolts and cunning keys.
One hears no whisper, rustle, thump, or thud.
Only the snow creaks. All men sleep. Dawn comes
not soon. All jails and locks have lapsed in sleep.
The iron weights in the fish-shop are asleep.
The carcasses of pigs sleep too. Backyards
and houses. Watch-dogs in their chains lie cold.
In cellars sleeping cats hold up their ears.
Mice sleep, and men. And London soundly sleeps.
A schooner nods at anchor. The salt sea
talks in its sleep with snow beneath her hull,
and melts into the distant sleeping sky.
John Donne has sunk in sleep, with him the sea.
Chalk cliffs now tower in sleep above the sands.
This island sleeps, embraced by lonely dreams,
and every garden now is triple-barred.
Pines, maples, birches, firs, and spruce—all sleep.
On mountain slopes steep mountain-streams and paths
now sleep. Foxes and wolves. Bears in their dens.
The snow drifts high at burrow-entrances.
All the birds sleep. Their songs are heard no more.
Nor is the crow's hoarse *caw.* At night the owl's
dark hollow laugh is quenched. The open fields
of England now are stilled. A clear star flames.
The mice are penitent. All creatures sleep.
The dead lie calmly in their graves and dream.
The living, in the oceans of their gowns,
sleep—each alone—within their beds. Or two
by two. Hills, woods, and rivers sleep. All birds
and beasts now sleep—nature alive and dead.
But still the snow spins white from the black sky.
There, high above men's heads, all are asleep.
The angels sleep. Saints—to their saintly shame—

have quite forgotten this our anxious world.
Dark Hell-fires sleep, and glorious Paradise.
No one goes forth from home at this bleak hour.
Even God has gone to sleep. Earth is estranged.
Eyes do not see, and ears perceive no sound.
The Devil sleeps. Harsh enmity has fallen
asleep with him on snowy English fields.
All horsemen sleep.[1] And the Archangel, with
his trumpet. Horses, softly swaying, sleep.
And all the cherubim, in one great host
embracing, doze beneath St. Paul's high dome.
John Donne has sunk in sleep. His verses sleep.
His images, his rhymes, and his strong lines
fade out of view. Anxiety and sin,
alike grown slack, sleep in his syllables.
And each verse whispers to its next of kin,
'Move on a bit.' But each stands so remote
from Heaven's Gates, so poor, so pure and dense,
that all seems one. All are asleep. The vault
austere of iambs soars in sleep. Like guards,
the trochees stand and nod to left and right.
The vision of Lethean waters sleeps.
The poet's fame sleeps soundly at its side.
All trials, all sufferings, are sunk in sleep.
And vices sleep. Good lies in Evil's arms.
The prophets sleep. The bleaching snow seeks out,
through endless space, the last unwhitened spot.
All things have lapsed in sleep. The swarms of books,
the streams of words, cloaked in oblivion's ice,
sleep soundly. Every speech, each speech's truth,
is sleeping. Linked chains, sleeping scarcely clank.
All soundly sleep: the saints, the Devil, God.
Their wicked and their faithful servants. Snow
alone sifts, rustling, on the darkened roads.
And there are no more sounds in all the world.

---

1   This allusion is both to the English knights who fought in the War of the Roses and to
    the Four Horsemen of the Apocalypse.—G. K.

But hark! Do you not hear in the chill night
a sound of sobbing, whisperings of fear?
There someone stands, disclosed to winter's blast,
and weeps. There someone stands in the dense gloom.
His voice is thin. His voice is needle-thin,
yet without tread. And he in solitude
swims through the falling snow—cloaked in cold mist –
that stiches night to dawn. The lofty dawn.
'Whose sobs are those? My angel, is it you?
Do you await my coming, there alone
beneath the snow? Walking—without my love—
in darkness home? Do you cry in the gloom?'
No answer.—'Is it you, o cherubim,
whose muted tears put me in mind
of some sepulchral choir? Have you resolved
to quit my sleeping church? Is it not you?'
No answer.—'Is it you, o Paul? Your voice
most certainly is coarsened by stern speech.
Have you not bowed your grey head in the gloom
to weep?' But only silence makes reply.
'Is that the Hand which looms up everywhere
to shield a grieving glance in the deep dark?
Is it not thou, Lord? No, my thoughts run wild.
And yet how lofty is the voice that weeps.'
No answer. Silence.—'Gabriel, have you
not blown your trumpet to the roar of hounds?
Why did I stand alone with open eyes
while horsemen saddled their swift steeds? Yet each
thing sleeps. Enveloped in huge gloom, the Hounds
of Heaven race in packs. O Gabriel,
do you not sob, encompassèd about
by winter dark, alone, with your great horn?'

'No, it is I, your soul, John Donne, who speaks.
I grieve alone upon the heights of Heaven,
because my labors did bring forth to life
feelings and thoughts as heavy as stark chains.
Bearing this burden, you could yet fly up
past those dark sins and passions, mounting higher.

You were a bird, your people did you see
in every place, as you did soar above
their sloping roofs. And you did glimpse the seas,
and distant lands, and Hell—first in your dreams,
then waking. You did see a jewelled Heaven
set in the wretched frame of men's low lusts.
And you saw Life: your Island was its twin.
And you did face the ocean at its shores.
The howling dark stood close at every hand.
And you did soar past God, and then drop back,
for this harsh burden would not let you rise
to that high vantage point from which this world
seems naught but ribboned rivers and tall towers—
that point from which, to him who downward stares,
this dread Last Judgement seems no longer dread.
The radiance of that Country does not fade.
From there all here seems a faint, fevered dream.
From there our Lord is but a light that gleams,
through fog, in window of the farthest house.
The fields lie fallow, furrowed by no plough.
The years lie fallow, and the centuries.
Forests alone stand, like a steady wall.
Rain batters the high head of giant grass.
The first woodcutter—he whose withered mount,
in panic fear of thickets, blundered thence—
will climb a pine to catch a sudden glimpse
of fires in his own valley, far away.
All things are distant. What is near is dim.
The level glance slides from a roof remote.
All here is bright. No din of baying hound
or tolling bell disturbs the silent air.
And, sensing that all things are far away,
he'll wheel his horse back quickly toward the woods.
And instantly, reins, sledge, night, his poor mount,
himself—will melt into a Scriptural dream.
But here I stand and weep. The road is gone.
I am condemned to live among these stones.
I cannot fly up in my body's flesh;

such flight at best will come to me through death
in the wet earth, when I've forgotten you,
my world, forgotten you once and for all.
I'll follow, in the torment of desire,
to stitch this parting up with my own flesh.
But listen! While with weeping I disturb
your rest, the busy snow whirls through the dark,
not melting, as it stitches up this hurt—
its needles flying back and forth, back, forth!
It is not I who sob. It's you, John Donne:
you lie alone. Your pans in cupboards sleep,
while snow builds drifts upon your sleeping house—
while snow sifts down to earth from highest Heaven.'

Like some great bird, he sleeps in his own nest,
his pure path and his thirst for purer life,
himself entrusting to that steady star
which now is closed in clouds. And like a bird,
his soul is pure, and his life's path on earth,
although it needs must wind through sin, is still
closer to nature than that tall crow's nest
which soars above the starlings' empty homes.
Like some great bird, he too will wake at dawn;
but now he lies beneath a veil of white,
while snow and sleep stitch up the throbbing void
between his soul and his own dreaming flesh.
All things have sunk in sleep. But one last verse
awaits its end, baring its fangs to snarl
that carnal love is but a poet's duty—
spiritual love the essence of a priest.
Whatever millstone these swift waters turn
will grind the same coarse grain in this one world.
For though our life may be a thing to share,
who is there in this world to share our death?
Man's garment gapes with holes. It can be torn,
by him who will, at this edge or at that.
It falls to shreds and is made whole again.
Once more it's rent. And only the far sky,

in darkness, brings the healing needle home.
Sleep, John Donne, sleep. Sleep soundly, do not fret
your soul. As for your coat, it's torn; all limp
it hangs. But see, there from the clouds will shine
that Star which made your world endure till now.

1963

Nunc Dimittis[2]

When Mary first came to present the Christ Child
to God in His temple, she found—of those few
who fasted and prayed there, departing not from it—
    devout Simeon and the prophetess Anna.

The holy man took the Babe up in his arms.
The three of them, lost in the grayness of dawn,
now stood like a small shifting frame that surrounded
    the Child in the palpable dark of the temple.

The temple enclosed them in forests of stone.
Its lofty vaults stooped as though trying to cloak
the prophetess Anna, and Simeon, and Mary—
    to hide them from men and to hide them from Heaven.

And only a chance ray of light struck the hair
of that sleeping Infant, who stirred but as yet
was conscious of nothing and blew drowsy bubbles;
    old Simeon's arms held him like a stout cradle.

It had been revealed to this upright old man
that he would not die until his eyes had seen

---

2   This poem—titled in the original "Sreten′e" [The Presentation (in the Temple)]—is based on the account in Luke 2:22–36, which Brodsky considers the point of transition from the Old Testament to the New. Simeon's speech in the fifth and sixth stanzas, the "Nunc dimittis" ("Now lettest thou thy servant depart . . ."), is found in most Christian liturgies. —G.K.

the Son of the Lord. And it thus came to pass. And
    he said: 'Now, O Lord, lettest thou thy poor servant,

according to thy holy word, leave in peace,
for mine eyes have witnessed thine offspring, he is
thy continuation and also the source of
    thy Light for idolatrous tribes, and the glory

of Israel as well.' Then old Simeon paused.
The silence, regaining the temple's clear space,
oozed from all its corners and almost engulfed them,
    and only his echoing words grazed the rafters,

to spin for a moment, with faint rustling sounds,
high over their heads in the tall temple's vaults,
akin to a bird that can soar, yet that cannot
    return to the earth, even if it should want to.

A strangeness engulfed them. The silence now seemed
as strange as the words of old Simeon's speech.
And Mary, confused and bewildered, said nothing—
    so strange had his words been. He added, while turning

directly to Mary: 'Behold, in this Child,
now close to thy breast, is concealed the great fall
of many, the great elevation of others,
    a subject of strife and a source of dissension,

and that very steel which will torture his flesh
shall pierce through thine own soul as well. And that wound
will show to thee, Mary, as a new vision,
    what lies hidden, deep in the hearts of all people.'

He ended and moved toward the temple's great door.
Old Anna, bent down with the weight of her years,
and Mary, now stooping, gazed after him, silent.
    He moved and grew smaller, in size and in meaning,

to these two frail women who stood in the gloom.
As though driven on by the force of their looks,
he strode through the cold empty space of the temple
    and moved toward the whitening blur of the doorway.

The stride of his old legs was steady and firm.
When Anna's voice sounded behind him, he slowed
his step for a moment. But she was not calling
    to him; she had started to bless God and praise Him.

The door came still closer. The wind stirred his robe
and fanned at his forehead; the roar of the street,
exploding in life by the door of the temple,
    beat stubbornly into old Simeon's hearing.

He went forth to die. It was not the loud din
of streets that he faced when he flung the door wide,
but rather the deaf-and-dumb fields of death's kingdom.
    He strode through a space that was no longer solid.

The rustle of time ebbed away in his ears.
And Simeon's soul held the form of the Child—
its feathery crown now enveloped in glory—
    aloft, like a torch, pressing back the black shadows,

to light up the path that leads into death's realm,
where never before until this present hour
had any man managed to lighten his pathway.
    The old man's torch glowed and the pathway grew wider.

February 16, 1972[3]

---

3   The date February 16 (on the New Calendar; or February 3 on the Old) is the Feast Day
of Saints Simeon and Anna, and hence the name day of Anna Akhmatova—a point
which Brodsky wishes to emphasize.—G. K.

Odysseus to Telemachus

My dear Telemachus,
          The Trojan War
is over now; I don't recall who won it.
The Greeks, no doubt, for only they would leave
so many dead so far from their own homeland.
But still, my homeward way has proved too long.
While we were wasting time there, old Poseidon,
it almost seems, stretched and extended space.

I don't know where I am or what this place
can be. It would appear some filthy island,
with bushes, buildings, and great grunting pigs.
A garden choked with weeds; some queen or other.
Grass and huge stones . . . Telemachus, my son!
To a wanderer the faces of all islands
resemble one another. And the mind
trips, numbering waves; eyes, sore from sea horizons,
run; and the flesh of water stuffs the ears.
I can't remember how the war came out;
even how old you are—I can't remember.

Grow up, then, my Telemachus, grow strong.
Only the gods know if we'll see each other
again. You've long since ceased to be that babe
before whom I reined in the plowing bullocks.
Had it not been for Palamedes' trick
we two would still be living in one household.
But maybe he was right; away from me
you are quite safe from all Oedipal passions,
and your dreams, my Telemachus, are blameless.

[March] 1972

The Butterfly

I

Should I say that you're dead?
You touched so brief a fragment
of time. There's much that's sad in
the joke God played.
I scarcely comprehend
the words "you've lived"; the date of
your birth and when you faded
in my cupped hand
are one, and not two dates.
Thus calculated,
your term is, simply stated,
less than a day.

II

It's clear that days for us
are nothings, zeros.
They can't be pinned down near us
to feed our eyes.
Whenever days stand stark
against white borders,
since they possess no bodies
they leave no mark.
They are like you. That is,
each butterfly's small plumage
is one day's shrunken image—
a tenth its size.

III

Should I say that, somehow,
you lack all being?
What then, are my hands feeling
that's so like you?
Such colors can't be drawn
from nonexistence.
Tell me, at whose insistence
were yours laid on?
Since I'm a mumbling heap
of words, not pigments,
how could your hues be figments
of my conceit?

IV

There are, on your small wings,
black spots and splashes—
like eyes, birds, girls, eyelashes.
But of what things
are you the airy norm?
What bits of faces,
what broken times and places
shine through your form?
As for your *nature mortes*:
do they show dishes
of fruits and flowers, or fishes
displayed on boards?

V

Perhaps a landscape smokes
among your ashes,
and with thick reading glasses
I'll scan its slopes—
its beaches, dancers, nymphs.
Is it as bright as

the day, or dark as night is?
And could one glimpse—
ascending that sky's screen—
some blazing lantern?
And tell me, please, what pattern
inspired this scene?

VI

It seems to me you are
a protean creature,
whose markings mask a feature
of face, or stone, or star.
Who was the jeweler,
brow uncontracted,
who from our world extracted
your miniature—
a world where madness brings
us low, and lower,
where we are things, while you are
the thought of things?

VII

Why were these lovely shapes
and colors given
for your one day of life in
this land of lakes?
—a land whose dappled mir-
rors have one merit:
reflecting space, they store it.
Such brief existence tore
away your chance
to be captured, delivered,
within cupped hands to quiver—
the hunter's eye entrance.

VIII

You shun every response—
but not from shyness
or wickedness or slyness,
and not because
you're dead. Dead or alive,
to God's least creature
is given voice for speech, or
for song—a sign
that it has found a way
to bind together,
and stretch life's limits, whether
an hour or day.

IX

But you lack even this:
the means to utter
a word. Yet, probe the matter;
it's better thus.
You're not in heaven's debt,
on heaven's ledger.
It's not a curse, I pledge you,
that your small weight
and span rob you of tongue.
Sound's burden, too, is grievous.
And you're more speechless,
less fleshed, than time.

X

Living too brief an hour
for fear or trembling,
you spin, motelike, ascending
above this bed of flowers,
beyond the prison space
where past and future

combine to break, or batter,
our lives, and thus
when your path leads you far
to open meadows,
your pulsing wings bring shadows
and shapes to air.

XI

So, too, the sliding pen
which inks a surface
has no sense of the purpose
of any line
or that the whole will end
as an amalgam
of heresy and wisdom;
it therefore trusts the hand
whose silent speech incites
fingers to throbbing—
whose spasm reaps no pollen,
but eases hearts.

XII

Such beauty, set beside
so brief a season,
suggests to our stunned reason
this bleak surmise:
the world was made to hold
no end or *telos*,
and if—as some would tell us—
there is a goal,
it's not ourselves.
No butterfly collector
can trap light or detect where
the darkness dwells.

XIII

Should I bid you farewell
as to a day that's over?
Men's memories may wither,
grow thin, and fall
like hair. The trouble is,
behind their backs are:
not double beds for lovers,
hard sleep, the past,
or days in shrinking files
backstretched—but, rather,
huge clouds, circling together,
of butterflies.

XIV

You're better than No-thing.
That is, you're nearer,
more reachable, and clearer.
Yet you're akin
to nothingness—
like it, you're wholly empty.
And if, in your life's venture,
No-thing takes flesh,
that flesh will die.
Yet while you live you offer
a frail and shifting buffer,
dividing it from me.

1973

Chapter 10

In Memory of a Poet: Variation on a Theme[1]

by Tomas Venclova
(trans. George L. Kline)

В Петербурге мы сойдемся снова.

Osip Mandelstam[2]

Did you regain this promised place, revisit
This skeleton, this bare map, of a city?
The Admiralty spire sinks through the blizzard;[3]
The geometric paint on level squares
Turns pale.

---

1   George L. Kline is known for his translations of Joseph Brodsky, but he also translated poems by Anna Akhmatova, Boris Pasternak, Marina Tsvetaeva, and others. This unpublished translation of the eminent European poet Tomas Venclova's "Poeto Atminimui. Variantas," in which Kline was assisted by Romuald Misiunas and Audrone Kubilius-Misiunas, was found among Kline's papers. I would like to thank the Kline Estate for its permission to publish the poem here. There are a number of notations on the draft—footnotes with alternative suggestions are included here to illustrate his translation choices. The poem is republished with the generous permission of Tomas Venclova.—C.L.H.

2   Kline's draft translation omits the epigraph from Osip Mandelstam: "We'll come together again in Petersburg."

3   Or ". . . melts in the blizzard"—G. K.

Electric power is disconnected,
A shade emerges from its icy spectrum;
Behind Izmailov Boulevard a specter
Of rusty locomotives looms and stares

This streetcar is the same, this threadbare topcoat . . .
A scrap of paper spins above the asphalt,
The nineteenth century's enormous icefloe
Blocks off the station's stream.
                    The roaring sky
Slams shut. The decades fade and lose their features,
The clouded cities blow past like bad weather;
There is a kind of gift in echoed gestures,[4]
But no man's ever born a second time.

He draws back to the February morning
Which grips this slow and sluggish northern Rome, and
Moves off to test a different horizon,
Whose rhythms reproduce the beat of snow.
He's called to wolf-caves where the tense walls glisten,
To mental hospitals, to dirt, to prison,
To Petersburg's bleak, black familiar vision,
At which his words were pointed long ago.

There's no rebirth of harmony or measure.
But time has kindled, in the world's wide brazier,
A fire of ticking logs; still its own treasure[5]
Lies lower, in a timeless hearth, which warms
And focuses our fate with clean-edged lenses
That bring to light a web of happy chances
And sometimes make our doings strong events, as
Finite extensions of eternal forms.[6]

---

4   Or "There's something gift-like in repeated gestures"—G. K.
5   Or "A fire of clacking logs . . ." (avoiding the clichéd expression "crackling logs")—G. K.
6   Or "Continuations of . . ."—G. K.

Reality—not mirrored, interrupted—
An island that has rivered, foamed, erupted,
To take the place of Paradise Disrupted,[7]
And batter through the shell of living speech.
Against a flood of clouds above the ark's bow
White doves describe a giant circle, doubtful
Of their own power to pick out, or to vouch for,
Mount Ararat among its neighbor peeks.

Cast off from shore! Set sail! The hour's upon us.
Stones split; the lie runs out. We have among us
But one remaining witness: art alone is
A light to break our midnight winterdrift.[8]
Black ice is overwhelmed by blessed grasses,
Dark rivers rub the sea with their wet noses,
A meaningless, unweighted, lost word splashes—
A word almost as meaningless as death.

---

7 Or ". . . of Paradise, disrupt it"—G. K.
8 Or "A spark to torch our . . ."—G. K.

Chapter 11

Occasional Poems: George Kline, Joseph Brodsky

Joseph Brodsky and George Kline enjoyed birthdays. This letter to a mailing list on April 23, 1970, honored Brodsky's May 24 birthday in Leningrad:

To Joseph Brodsky's Friends and Well-Wishers:

On May 24, 1970, Joseph (Iosif) will celebrate his thirtieth birthday. I know that remembrances from his friends and admirers abroad will mean a great deal to him.

May I suggest that you send him a congratulatory cable, card, or note (allowing two weeks for airmail from Europe, and three weeks for airmail from the United States) to the following address:

Mr. Joseph Brodsky   CCCP
24 Liteiny Prospekt, Apt. 28   Ленинград Д-28
Leningrad D-28   Литейный проспект, д. 24, кв. 28
USSR   Бродскому И. А.

I am sending this reminder to only a dozen or fifteen people; I urge each of you to keep the address confidential.

Cordially,
George L. Kline

The following year, the year before Brodsky's exile, he sent this telegram on May 23, 1971, from Ardmore, Pennsylvania:

> WHEN YOU WERE ONE, I WAS TWENTY TIMES YOUR AGE, BUT NOW THAT YOU ARE 31, ONLY 1.6 TIMES. CLEARLY I GROW YOUNGER AS YOU GROW OLDER. AFFECTIONATELY, GEORGE

Brodsky frequently spent his Christmases in Italy. In 1975, Kline sent him this holiday greeting to Venice by mailgram:

According to the New York Times,
Wet Venice has been saved from sinking.
So let your spirits with her climb,
While light heads banish heavy thinking.

Affectionate wishes for Christmas and New Years
George

Below, Kline's poem on Brodsky's fiftieth birthday in 1990.

To Joseph on Turning Fifty

S liubov'iu

If we take *years* to be the way
a life is measured, then—ok—
yours now stands firm at *piat'desiat.*
But if it's *months* we're looking at,
seicento is the sum; and cal-
ibrating a life's calendar
in *weeks* yields *due mila e
seicento.* Put such sums away!
Judge lives by daunting tasks achieved,
by honest thoughts and decent deeds,
and then the number has no limit:
the life holds *endlessness* within it.

May 24, 1990

Brodsky returned the favor with more levity on the occasion of Kline's retirement party at Bryn Mawr the following year.

Festschrift for George L. Kline

(Somewhere in the sky between Bradley Field and Philadelphia)
April 19, 1991

He served in the US Air Force,
Studied and taught philosophies,
Translated me, of course—
For fun, not, alas, for colossal fees.
It's a moment of great solemnity!
At seventy, ah, at seventy
One switches from coffee to lemon tea,
Thoughts acquire serenity
And the sharpness of peaks in Yosemity,
Gravity yields to levity.
And it's an insane obscenity
to say that seventy's too late
For enterprise or passion:
Just watch our George translate
From Russian.
As he is from Bryn Mawr
His motto, of course, is "Bring more!"

Chapter 12

A Bibliography of George Kline's Published Translations of Joseph Brodsky's Poems

1965

1. "New Poems by Joseph Brodsky" ["Elegy for John Donne"; "A Christmas Ballad"; "That evening sprawling by an open fire"; "Solitude"; "Sadly and Tenderly"; "They served us noodles one more time, and you . . ."] (with introductory note), *TriQuarterly* 3 (Spring 1965): 85–96. Also includes Andrei Voznesensky's "Oza": 97–117.
2. "'Elegy for John Donne' by Joseph Brodsky" (with introductory essay), *Russian Review* 24, no. 4 October (1965): 341–53.

1966

3. "Three Poems by Brodsky" ["The Pushkin Monument," "Pilgrims," "To Gleb Gorbovsky"], *Russian Review* 25 (April 1966): 131–34.

1968

4. "Joseph Brodsky's 'Verses on the Death of T. S. Eliot'" (with introductory note), *Russian Review* 27 (April 1968): 195–98.

"Joseph Brodsky's Six New Poems" ["To Lycomedes on Scyros," "Washerwoman Bridge," "Sonnet ('How Sad that My Life Has not Come to Mean . . .')," "Verses on the Death T. S. Eliot," "The Fountain," "A Stopping Place in the Wilderness"] (with introductory essay), *Unicorn Journal*, no. 2 (1968): 20–30.

1970

5. "Joseph Brodsky's 'A Winter Evening in Yalta,'" *The Observer Review* [London], January 11 1970, 29.
6. "Two Poems by Joseph Brodsky" ["A Prophecy" and "Two Hours Down by the Reservoir"] in *Explorations in Freedom: Prose, Narrative, and Poetry from Kultura*, ed. Leopold Tyrmand, (New York: The Free Press in cooperation with The State University of New York at Albany, 1970), 265–70.
7. Joseph Brodsky's "Now that I've walled myself off from the world . . . ," *The Third Hour,* no. 9 (1970).
8. "Five Poems by Joseph Brodsky" ["Almost an Elegy," "Enigma for an Angel," "Stanzas ('Let our farewell be silent . . .'), "You'll flutter, robin redbreast . . . ," "The Candlestick"], *TriQuarterly* 18 (Spring 1970): 175–83.

1971

9. "Joseph Brodsky's "Adieu, Mademoiselle Véronique" (with introductory note), *Russian Review* 30 (January 1971): 27–32.
10. "Three Poems by Joseph Brodsky" ["Verses in April," "September First," "Sonnet ('Once more we're living as by Naples Bay . . .'), *Arroy* [Bryn Mawr literary review] (May 1971): 2–4.
11. "Six Poems by Joseph Brodsky" ["Aeneas and Dido," "I bent to kiss your shoulders and I saw . . . ," "The trees in my window, in my wooden-framed window . . . ," "The fire as you can hear is dying down . . . ," "January 1, 1965," and "A Letter in a Bottle"], *Russian Literature TriQuarterly*, no. 1 (Fall 1971): 76–90.

1972

12. "Eight Poems by Joseph Brodsky" ["Sonnet ('The month of January has flown past . . .')", "You're coming home again. What does that mean?", "In

villages God does not live only . . . ," "Spring Season of Muddy Roads," "Exhaustion now is a more frequent guest . . . ," "Evening," "Refusing to catalogue all of one's woes . . . ," "Einem alten Architekten in Rom" (with introductory note), *Antaeus*, no. 6 (Summer 1972): 99–113.

13. "Joseph Brodsky's 'Nature Morte,'" *Saturday Review: The Arts* 55, no. 3 (August 12, 1972): 45.

14. "Eight Poems by Joseph Brodsky" ["A Halt in the Wilderness," "To a Certain Poetess," "Adieu," "Mademoiselle Véronique," "New Stanzas to Augusta," "Verses on the Death of T. S. Eliot," "The Fountain," "Post Aetatem Nostram," "Nature Morte"] (Russian texts on facing pages) in *The Living Mirror: Five Young Poets from Leningrad*, ed. Suzanne Massie (New York: Doubleday, 1972), 228–99.

15. "Three Poems by Joseph Brodsky" ["Two Hours in an Empty Tank," September the First," "Quilt-jacketed, a tree-surgeon . . ."], *New Leader* 55, no. 24 (December 11, 1972): 3–4.

1973

16. "Joseph Brodsky's 'The tenant finds his new house wholly strange . . . ,'" *The Nation*, January 1, 1973, 28.

17. "Three Poems by Joseph Brodsky" ["The days glide over me . . .," "In villages God does not live only . . . ," and *from* Gorbunov and Gorchakov, canto X: "And silence is the future of all days . . ."] (with introductory essay), *Mademoiselle* 76, no. 4 (February 1973): 138–39, 188–90.

18. "Three Poems by Joseph Brodsky"[*from* The School Anthology: Albert Frolov, Odysseus to Telemachus; and *from* Gorbunov and Gorchakov, canto II] (with introductory essay), *New York Review of Books*, April 5, 1973, 10–12.

19. "Joseph Brodsky's 'Dido and Aeneas,'" *Partisan Review* 40, no. 2 (1973): 255.

20. "Joseph Brodsky's 'Nunc Dimittis,'" *Vogue*, September 1973, 286–87.

21. "Joseph Brodsky's 'Dido and Aeneas,'" in Susan Jacoby, "Joseph Brodsky in Exile," *Change: The Magazine for Higher Learning* 5, no. 6 (Summer 1973): 68–63.

22. "Joseph Brodsky, 'Postscriptum,'" *New York Review of Books*, December 30, 1973.

23. *Joseph Brodsky: Selected Poems,* introduction and trans. by George Kline, foreword by W. H. Auden (Harmondsworth: Penguin Books, 1973).

1974

24. *Joseph Brodsky: Selected Poems,* introduction and trans. by George Kline, foreword by W. H. Auden (New York: Harper & Row, 1974; copyright 1973).
25. "Joseph Brodsky's 'An Autumn evening in the modest square . . . ,'" *Confrontation*, no. 8, (Spring 1974): 20–21.
26. "Joseph Brodsky's 'Letters to a Roman Friend,'" *Los Angeles Times*, June 16, 1974, pt. 5, p. 3.
27. "Joseph Brodsky's 'Nature Morte,'" *Post-War Russian Poetry*, ed. Daniel Weissbort (London: Penguin Books, 1974), 263–68.
28. "Joseph Brodsky's 'In the Lake District,'" *Alumnae Bulletin* [Bryn Mawr] (Fall 1974): 18.

1975

29. *Three Slavic Poets* (Chicago: Elpenor Books, 1975), George Kline's translation of "Dido and Aeneas" is included.

1976

30. "Josephs Brodsky's 'The Butterfly,'" *New Yorker*, March 15, 1976, 35.
31. "Three Poems by Joseph Brodsky" ["Sadly and Tenderly," "A Winter Evening In Yalta," and :A Prophecy"] in *The Contemporary World Poets*, ed. Donald Junkins (New York: Harcourt Brace Jovanovich, 1976), 268–71.
32. "Joseph Brodsky's 'In the Lake District' and 'On the Death of Zhukov,'" in *Kontinent*, (Garden City: Doubleday Anchor Books, 1976), 119–21. "In the Lake District" is reprinted from *Mademoiselle* 82, no. 5 (May 1976); an earlier version appeared in the Bryn Mawr *Alumnae Bulletin* (Fall 1974).

1977

33. "Two Poems by Joseph Brodsky" ["That evening, sprawling by an open fire . . . ," "Verses on the Death of T. S. Eliot"] in *Russian Writing Today*, ed. Robin Milner-Gulland and Martin Dewhirst (London: Penguin Books, 1977), 179–83.

34. "Joseph Brodsky's 'A second Christmas by the shore . . . ,'" *Paintbrush* 4, no. 7–8 (1977): 27.

1979

35. "Joseph Brodsky's 'Plato Elaborated,'" *New Yorker,* March 12, 1979, 40–41.

1980

36. Joseph Brodsky *A Part of Speech,* trans. various hands (New York: Farrar, Straus, and Giroux, 1980). George Kline translated ten poems: "The Second Christmas by the Shore," "Nature Morte," "Letters to a Roman Friend," "Nunc Dimittis," "Odysseus to Telemachus," "An autumn evening in the modest square . . . ," "In the Lake District," "The Butterfly," "On the Death of Zhukov," "Plato Elaborated."

1981

37. "Joseph Brodsky's 'Odysseus to Telemachus,'" reprinted from *A Part of Speech* (New York: Farrar, Straus, and Giroux, 1981), 58, in Ruth Miller and Robert A. Greenberg, *Poetry: An Introduction* (New York: St. Martin's Press, 1981), 372.

1982

38. 'Joseph Brodsky's 'December in Florence'" (with Maurice English), *Shearsman,* no. 7 (1982): 19–21.

1985

39. Joseph Brodsky, "Enigma for an Angel," Stanzas: ("Let our farewell be silent . . ."), *TriQuarterly,* no 63 (Spring 1985), reprinted from *TriQuarterly,* no. 18 (Spring 1970).

1987

40. "Joseph Brodsky's Eclogue V: Summer" (with the author), *New Yorker,* August 3, 1987, 22–24.

1988

41. "Joseph Brodsky's Eclogue V: Summer" (with the author), in his book *To Urania* [poems translated by various hands] (New York: Farrar, Straus, and Giroux, 1988), 82–89.
42. Joseph Brodsky, "The Butterfly," Alumnae Bulletin, LXIX, no. 2 [Bryn Mawr] (Winter 1988): 19

1989

43. "Joseph Brodsky's Advice to a Traveller" (with the author), *Times Literary Supplement,* May 12–18, 1989, 5–6.
44. "Joseph Brodsky's 'Eclogue V: Summer'" (with the author) in the collection *To Urania* [poems translated by various hands] (Oxford: Oxford University Press, 1989), 82–89

1991

45. Joseph Brodsky, "Advice to a Traveller" (with the author), in *Worst Journeys: The Picador Book of Travel,* ed. Keath Fraser (New York: Vintage Books, 1991), 3–6.

1993

46. Joseph Brodsky, "Nature Morte," in *Twentieth Century Russian Poetry: Silver and Steel: An Anthology,* selected and introduced by Yevgeny Yevtushenko, ed. A. C. Todd and Max Hayward with Daniel Weissbort (New York: Doubleday, 1993), 960–64.

1996

47. Joseph Brodsky, *So Forth* [poems translated by various hands] (New York: Farrar, Straus, and Giroux, 1996), —Kline's translation (with the author) of Joseph Brodsky's "An Admonition" is on pp. 16–20.

2000

48. Joseph Brodsky, *Collected Poems in English* (New York: Farrar, Straus and Giroux, 2000), translations by various hands. The following Brodsky

poems translated by George Kline are included: "A second Christmas by the shore . . . ," 10–11; "Nature Morte," 48–52; "Letters to a Roman Friend," 58–60; "Nunc Dimittis," 61–63; "An autumn evening in the modest square . . . ," 65–66; "In the Lake District," 71; "The Butterfly," 72–77; "On the Death of Zhukov," 85–86; "Plato Elaborated," 140–42; "Eclogue V: Summer," 295–302; "An Admonition," 356–59. "Brodsky's *Presepio* in the Context of His Other Nativity Poems," *Symposion: A Journal of Russian Thought* 7–12 (2002–7): 67–80.

2020

49. Joseph Brodsky, *Selected Poems, 1968–1996,* edited by Ann Kjellberg (New York, Farrar, Straus & Giroux, 2020). The following Brodsky poems translated by George Kline are included: "Nature Morte," "Nunc Dimittis," "An autumn evening in the modest square...," "In the Lake District," "The Butterfly," "Plato Elaborated."

Compiled by Valentina Polukhina

Chapter 13

George L. Kline Chronology

1921—George Louis Kline is born in Galesburg, Illinois, on March 3, to Allen Sides Kline and Wahneta Burner Kline.

1938-41—Kline attends Boston University for three years, but then interrupts his education to enlist in the United States Army Air Corps. He becomes a lead navigator and bombardier in B-24s.

1943—Kline marries Virginia Harrington "Ginny" Hardy (born October 28, 1918) on April 17 in a simple civil ceremony where he is stationed in Texas.

1944—Between February and July, he flies a total of fifty combat missions out of Italy, for which he receives the Distinguished Flying Cross.

1946—Brenda "Bunny" Marie Kline is born July 16.

1947—Kline completes his BA (Hons) at Columbia College and begins graduate work in Slavic Studies, only later turning to philosophy. He begins his "love affair" with Russian poetry, and at some time during his graduate years, begins translating Pushkin. He publishes a short story by Mikhail Zoschenko.

1948—Kline receives an MA in philosophy from Columbia University. Jeffrey Allen Kline is born October 14.

1949—Kline publishes his first two works: "Dostoevsky's Grand Inquisitor and the Soviet Regime," *Occidental*, no. 2 (1949): 1–5 and "A Note on Soviet Logic," *Journal of Philosophy* 46 (1949): 228

1950—Kline receives his PhD in philosophy at Columbia University, with a dissertation titled *Spinoza in Soviet Philosophy* (published in 1952).

1950-52—Kline teaches philosophy at Columbia University.

1952-53—Kline is visiting assistant professor at the University of Chicago, where he first teaches Russian Ethical and Social Theory, which he was subsequently to teach many times over the course of his career. He also teaches Great Books of the Western World from Homer to Dostoevsky.

1953—He publishes English translation of V. V. Zenkovskii's two-volume *History of Russian Philosophy* (New York: Columbia University Press, 1953).

1953-59—Kline returns to teach at Columbia.

1955—Christina Hardy Kline is born March 15.

1956—Kline makes his first visit to Russia.

1957—Kline makes his second visit to Russia and is tailed by the KGB.

1959—Kline joins the faculty of Bryn Mawr College. For the first four years he teaches in both the philosophy and the Russian departments before settling in philosophy, where he becomes a full professor in 1966 and Milton C. Nahm Professor of Philosophy in 1981. In 1959, he also publishes translations of two early poems by Pasternak.

He also teaches one-semester courses at Rutgers, Johns Hopkins, the University of Pennsylvania, Haverford College, and Swarthmore College.

1960—Kline spends six weeks in the Soviet Union from July 3 to August 14, followed by his first visit to Poland on September 14-18, where he meets Leszek Kołakowski. He confronts a KGB agent in a Moscow hotel and is trailed by KGB agents on a four-hour drive from Warsaw to Kraków.

1964—Brodsky's trial is conducted in two segments on February 14 and March 13. He is charged with vagrancy, the distribution of works by forbidden authors (e.g., Akhmatova and Tsvetaeva), and the corruption of youth. He is further charged with "having a worldview damaging to the state, decadence, and modernism, failure to finish school, and social parasitism . . . except for the writing of awful poems." He is sentenced to five years' internal exile in a *sovkhoz*. He is held in a Leningrad psychiatric hospital and a prison complex. On March 25, he is sent to the village of Norenskaya near the Arctic Circle for manual labor.

Kline encounters the young Joseph Brodsky's poems in August, when they were published with a transcript of his trial in *The New Leader*. In December, a Polish scholar in Warsaw shows him Brodsky's 1963 poem "The Great Elegy for John Donne." He returns to Bryn Mawr by the end of the year, after a two-month stay in Eastern Europe.

1965—Brodsky's sentence is commuted, after international protests spearheaded by Akhmatova.

With others, Kline publishes *Russian Philosophy* (Quadrangle Books), a three-volume anthology of original translations of Russian philosophy texts, continuously in print from 1965 to the present and used in university classrooms. Although he is the de facto editor in chief for the influential work, he is named only as a "collaborator" to give prominence to the three younger scholars involved in the work.

In February, he receives a copy of "The Great Elegy for John Donne" from his colleague Vera Sandomirsky Dunham and translates it within weeks. It is published, with several shorter poems, in *TriQuarterly* [Northwestern University], no. 3 (Spring 1965).

The 1965 translated collection, *Iosif Brodskii, Stikhotvoreniia i poemy*, is published from a smuggled samizdat manuscript that has been gathered by Konstantin Kuzminsky and Grigory Kovalev. Gleb Struve and Boris Filipoff are the co-editors in the United States. The 239-page book is published by the Inter-Language Literary Associates of Washington and New York.

1966—He leaves for Russia July 9, but cuts his planned four-week visit short because of his twenty-year-old daughter's illness, which will eventually be diagnosed as multiple sclerosis. He never reaches Leningrad, and so is unable to meet Brodsky. He returns to the United States on July 22.

1967—Kline returns to Russia and meets Brodsky in August. They meet almost daily for the next week, and for several days when he returns to Leningrad in early September. They are trailed by the KGB.

Elegy to John Donne and Other Poems, translated by Lord Nicholas Bethell, is published in London. It is Brodsky's first collection in English, published without his knowledge or permission.

1968—Kline publishes *Religious and Anti-Religious Thought in Russia: The Weil Lectures* (Chicago: University of Chicago Press, 1968), which is nominated for Phi Beta Kappa's Ralph Waldo Emerson award. He visits Russia from June 11 to June 27. Brodsky insists he wants to have a Russian and English collection *A Halt in the Desert* published abroad.

Kline is taken for interrogation by the KGB in Leningrad. He meets the same KGB agents again, this time during his June 27–29 visit to Kiev, before his return to the United States. He is threatened with more interrogations if he continues to associate with Brodsky, and he replies, "Ia mogu zhit′ bez Rossii"—"I can live without Russia." This is his last visit to Russia before the dissolution of the Soviet Union.

Kline smuggles Anatoly Naiman's foreword along with poems for *Ostanovka v pustyne* [A halt in the desert] out of the Soviet Union.

1969—*Boris Pasternak: Seven Poems* is published by Unicorn Press, Santa Barbara, in a small run of 1,000. The poems had been previously published in *Columbia University Forum*, *Russian Review*, and *Unicorn Folio*.

1970—After delays, *Ostanovka v pustyne* (A halt in the desert), the first book of poetry in which Brodsky is actively involved, is published in May by Izdatel'stvo Imeni Chekhova in New York. Kline is the unnamed co-editor, with Max Hayward. A revised edition was published by Ardis in 1988, with Kline named as co-editor.

W. H. Auden invites Kline to visit him at Kirchstetten, outside Vienna, on July 21, following Brodsky's letter to the English poet. Kline had met with Auden several times at the poet's New York City apartment, after an introduction by Prof. Arcady Nebolsine.

1972—Kline hears of Brodsky's imminent expulsion in late May. Brodsky leaves Russia forever on June 4. Moscow officials confiscate and impound his manuscripts before his flight to Vienna. He meets Auden in Kirchstetten and after a twelve-day stay he flies to England with Auden for London's Poetry International Festival. While in London, on June 6 Brodsky meets Nikos Stangos, poetry editor of Penguin.

Kline meets Brodsky for the first time in four years at Albany airport on July 21, to work on translations together at the Kline summer cottage in the Berkshires, in western Massachusetts. They collaborate through July 26.

He meets Brodsky at the Philadelphia airport on October 4 for a series of readings in Philadelphia and New York, including at the Academy for American Poets.

1973—Publication of *Joseph Brodsky: Selected Poems,* translated by George Kline, by Penguin in the UK and, in hardcover in the United States, by Harper & Row. Kline interviews Brodsky in *Vogue* in September.

1980—Publication of *A Part of Speech* by Farrar, Straus & Giroux. Ten of the translations are Kline's.

1987—The Nobel Prize in Literature 1987 is awarded to Joseph Brodsky "for an all-embracing authorship, imbued with clarity of thought and poetic intensity." Kline is invited to attend the awards ceremony and events on December 10-11.

1991—In January 1991, Kline visits Leningrad and Moscow, in connection with the first international conference on the life and work of Brodsky in Leningrad. He makes four more visits, the last in August 1993.

Kline retires from Bryn Mawr. Brodsky speaks at Kline's retirement symposium.

1995—Kline attends the last birthday party of Brodsky on May 24 in Brooklyn Heights.

1996—Brodsky dies on January 28 in Brooklyn Heights, New York City.

1999—The Association for Slavic, East European, and Eurasian Studies recognizes Kline for "Distinguished Contributions to Slavic Studies." The citation cites his remarkable scholarly career as a philosopher, translator, editor, and teacher, and calls particular attention to:

his extraordinary impact on his fellow scholars, many of whom have been his students. They recall his erudite, generous, and detailed comments on their papers and books, and the depth and wisdom he brought to his scholarship. Countless younger scholars consider themselves indebted to him for his judgment, encouragement, and guidance. We all stand in his debt, therefore, for helping us to appreciate the richness and depth of Russian philosophy and literature and for his long dedication to nurturing our field.

2014—Virginia Kline dies on April 5 in Anderson, South Carolina. George Kline dies on October 21 in Anderson, South Carolina.

Afterword

This book is among the first of its kind, blending in-depth research with a new and authoritative interpretation of the poetics, style, and ideas of one of the most influential poets to emerge out of post-Stalin Russia—Joseph Brodsky, the 1987 Nobel Prize-winner for Literature. It also examines the relationship between the poet and translator, in its closest details.

Brodsky was lucky with his translators, among them some first-rate poets: Anthony Hecht, Richard Wilbur, Derek Walcott. However, George Kline was the first of them to bring Brodsky to the West in the early years, introducing him to Anglophone readers. Kline managed to translate not just Brodsky's poetry, but also the poems of Pasternak, Akhmatova, Tsvetaeva, and Venclova extremely well. For years, Kline and Brodsky had a very cordial relationship. Kline's experiences echo those of my late husband, Daniel Weissbort. Joseph and Daniel were like brothers initially, but, after Brodsky corrected Daniel's translation of the cycle "A Part of Speech," Daniel refused to keep his name under the altered translation. Brodsky insisted on keeping the meter and rhyme of the original, which placed considerable demands on the translator—the effort bordered on intellectual athleticism, if not acrobatics.

Derek Walcott told me that he, Brodsky, and translator Barry Rubin once spent three hours translating one line in the poem "Letter to the Ming Dynasty." Many were convinced that Brodsky's poetry could not be adequately rendered in English at all. For example, the second of the "Twenty Sonnets to Mary Queen of Scots," eventually translated by Peter France with Brodsky for the *Collected Poems in English,* begins this way:

> The war to end all wars produced ground zero.
> The frying pan missed fat that missed pork chops.[1]

---

1   Joseph Brodsky, *Collected Poems in English,* ed. Ann Kjellberg (New York: Farrar, Straus and Giroux, 2000), 226.

France writes: "As for the poet's food, we may notice that Sonnet 2 refers literally to the food shortages of the postwar years, for which the womb-like pleasure of the cinema with gorgeous images of love and death provided compensation."[2] But the lines offered problems, as writer Igor Efimov wrote:

> When some of Brodsky's lines surface, it's ridiculous to think even about translating something like: "At the end of the great war, which was for life or death, whatever we had we fried without fat . . ." [V kontse bolshoi voiny ne na zhivot, / kogda chto bylo zharili bez sala . . .]." "Ne na zhivot" is not the belly but for life, and not only did they fry, but they slaughtered. He could create a metaphorical bouquet in a single line.[3]

As a consequence, Robert Hass, a United States poet laureate as well as a translator of Miłosz, said the translations of Brodsky's poems sound "like an eighteenth-century hack rewriting Shakespeare." Or more often, given Brodsky's unlimited admiration for Auden, like one of those "clever young Englishmen of indeterminate age down from the university and set to make a splash." In the *New Republic*, Hass decried the "fatal miscalculations of tone" that made reading Brodsky's poetry "like wandering through the ruins of what has been reported to be a noble building."[4]

The other peculiar feature of Russian literature, poetry included, is that for centuries writers and poets were the only opposition party, the only defenders of the ordinary people. So the state paid great attention to a writer's work, so much so that he or she could be arrested, exiled, killed, or driven to suicide. Beginning with Alexander Pushkin and continuing with Fyodor Dostoevsky, Osip Mandelstam, Marina Tsvetaeva, and then in the twentieth century with Irina Ratushinskaya, Natalya Gorbanevskaya, and finally Brodsky himself, persecution was rife, and continues down to the current regime. Russian history was and still is capable either of elevating you to world fame or kicking you into oblivion—or both.

---

2   Loseff and Polukhina, *Brodsky's Poetics and Aesthetics*, 101. Peter France alludes to the 1940 German film *Das Herz der Königin* starring the Swedish actress Zarah Leander, whose luminous portrayal of the doomed Scottish queen had mesmerized the young Brodsky. Directed by Carl Froelich and shot in the Tempelhof Studios in Berlin, the film's anti-British stance furthered the propaganda aims of Nazi Germany.

3   Polukhina, *Brodsky through the Eyes of His Contemporaries*, 2:111. Incidentally, the Russian "ne na zhivot" means not only "to the death," but "to slaughter."

4   Robert Hass, "Four Reviews," in *Twentieth Century Pleasures: Prose on Poetry* (New York: HarperCollins, 2000), 135, 137.

Brodsky holds a singular position in Russian literature, though the issues he addressed as a poet, essayist, and playwright were universal: life and death, love and betrayal, God and language. For Brodsky, however, language *was* God and everything was sacrificed for it: personal life, health, love, children, and fate itself. As early as 1968, he was convinced that he would receive the Nobel Prize. He was nominated as early as 1980, and he was finally awarded in 1987. And in 1991, he succeeded Mark Strand as poet laureate of the United States—the first poet laureate who had been born abroad.

George Kline understood Brodsky's worth and was extremely attentive to every element of his poems. This book is is a superb guide to further study of Brodsky's work for both translators and poets, as well as the general reader who loves poetry and is intoxicated by it. It is highly readable, reliable, and contains well-researched source material.

—*Valentina Polukhina*

Acknowledgements

Although this volume is short, the list of those who have helped me is long. My first and greatest thanks is to George Kline himself, who generously gave his time, energy, and commitment until the last months of his life. I also thank the Kline Estate, and particularly Christina Kline Hanak, for having trust and confidence in this stranger who telephoned after George's death in 2015.

I also owe a great debt of gratitude to Bryn Mawr College, which has put its support behind my book on George Kline, its eminent Milton C. Nahm Professor of Philosophy. Specifically, I wish to thank the Department of Philosophy, the Department of Russian, and the Office of the Provost, which provided financial assistance for publication. Bryn Mawr has stood behind the project from the outset, when Andrew Mellon Foundation funds, administered by Bryn Mawr, underwrote the initial efforts for transcriptions and archival research. Nona Smith, Bryn Mawr's Director of Sponsored Research, was a steady and invaluable guide from those earliest days to the present. Thanks also to Bryn Mawr's Special Collections, which shared its photos from Joseph Brodsky's early years in the United States.

I am deeply grateful to the British Academy for its research grant, which was absolutely essential for creating this book. Brodsky scholar Valentina Polukhina in London took this project under her wing, especially since it extends the work of her seminal volumes *Brodsky through the Eyes of His Contemporaries*, another endeavor sponsored by the British Academy. I also offer thanks for her permission to quote extensively from the papers of poet and translator Daniel Weissbort, her late husband.

I owe gratitude, as always, to the Joseph Brodsky Estate, for permission to republish poems and letters. Thanks to Austin Mueller of the Wylie Agency and also Farrar, Straus, & Giroux. Above all, I once again thank

Brodsky Estate executor Ann Kjellberg for many kindnesses and conversations over the years.

There were many additional permissions needed for an effort where George's words had to be augmented by his publications. Many thanks to *Modern Poetry in Translation*, and thanks also to the Estate of Anthony Hecht for permission to cite Hecht's correspondence.

I am grateful to Professor Maxim D. Shrayer of Boston College, editor of the Jews of Russia and Eastern Europe and Their Legacy series at Academic Studies Press, for his enthusiasm and confidence in this project, and acquisitions editor Ekaterina Yanduganova, who was by my side during the the editorial process, even when working ten international time zones away.

The Russian poet Irina Mashinski, a friend George often mentioned during our talks, has been a fellow traveler on this journey—a consultant on Russian prosody and an early reader of this manuscript. Thanks also to Zakhar Ishov, another friend of George's, met only posthumously. I am grateful to both.

Some personal thanks to Zoë Patrick, who has been a source for design and photo restoration for several books, including this one. Thanks to an old friend, Marc Ventresca, for advice at a critical time. I am grateful also to Gillian Berchowitz and Rick Huard for guidance. And also thanks to Mary Pope Osborne, a magnanimous champion of this book, and Hoover fellow Paul Caringella, whose gentle encouragement was much appreciated.

And finally, thanks to the Hoover Institution, where I was a Voegelin Fellow during a critical year during this project, and Stanford University's Division of Literatures, Cultures, and Languages, where I was a visiting scholar.

Producing this book was truly a "without borders" endeavor. Ekaterina Yanduganova, Kira Nemirovsky, Ilya Nikolaev, and I worked from opposite sides of the globe to preserve the intellectual and creative harvest of this quiet, decent, but remarkable man. George L. Kline devoted his life to Russian and Soviet philosophy, ethics, culture, religion, and of course poetry. He would have been pleased and honored to know how many twenty-first-century Russians would be involved in this effort to extend his legacy. *Bol'shoe spasibo* to all for hard work and camaraderie.